MW00460265

When a Nurse Prays

Jennifer Buettner, RN, BSN, CEN

CrossLink Publishing
RAPID CITY, SD

Buettner/CrossLink Publishing
1601 Mt. Rushmore Rd., Ste 3288
Rapid City, SD 57701
www.CrossLinkPublishing.com

When a Nurse Prays / Jennifer Buetner. —1st ed.
ISBN 978-1-63357-389-5
Libray of Congress Control Number: 2021933625

This book reflects the author's recollections of actual experiences. The names of some individuals have been changed to respect their privacy.

This book is dedicated to all healthcare heroes everywhere who have devoted their lives to the care of others. May God bless you daily and fill you with courage, compassion, strength, and wisdom.

Contents

Preface

We all have various gifts and talents that are meant for a specific purpose in this life. I recently realized God has been weaving lessons into my past to prepare me for a moment such as this. Throughout my childhood I naturally excelled in reading, writing, and art. At the young age of fifteen, I declared to my mother that I finally knew what I wanted to be when I grew up; I wanted to be a writer. However, my mom persuaded me to pick something more practical like being a nurse. Little did I know that God would set everything in place, so that I would have the gift of writing matched with the skills of nursing.

Even as I set out to write the things God has placed in my heart, some have encouraged me to compromise and be more politically correct or write so that this could be applied to all world religions to avoid offending anyone. I absolutely respect other people's beliefs. Religious freedom is the very foundation of our country. While many of these simple prayer concepts can be applied to many other religions, that is not what God has called me to do. While it may not be popular, obedience can be more powerful than sacrifice. In a world where everyone can be proud of their lifestyle choices, Christians don't have to be ashamed of their faith. Therefore, I seek the praise of God more than the praise of man. Act 20:24 states: "But I do not account my life of any value nor as precious to myself, if only I may finish my course and ministry that I received from Lord Jesus, to testify to the gospel of the grace of God." Through this prayer journey, I set out to do just that and use my God given gift of writing for His Glory for a time such as now. Life is too short, and our patients, friends, family, God's children, and you matter to God.

My hope is that you will be equipped, encouraged, and empowered to invite prayer into today's scientific equation for health and healing. God has given us the gifts of science and medicine; we should use them. However, we should also use one of the greatest gifts given to us, prayer. While many of these stories are related to my role as a nurse, we are all nurses if you think about it. If you have ever taken care of your spouse, mother, father, brother, sister, son, daughter, cousin, neighbor, friend, colleague, or stranger you too have been a nurse. With discussion questions and focused prayers at the end of each chapter, this book is perfect for small devotional study groups or for reading on your own or with your friends on your lunch break.

Acknowledgements

No book is written without the help of many people. I thank God for placing a few guiding lights in life to help me dive deeper into this spiritual journey. During a mission trip to Ecuador in 2016, it was a wise church elder, Scott Shade, who first suggested I write about my spiritual journey and the lessons I learned about prayer. Two years later it was a dear sister in faith, Meredith Wilson, who gave me the encouragement to do what God was calling me to do, despite my excuses and busy working mom schedule. I want to thank a few dear friends and sisters in faith who helped review chapters for edits and provide valuable feedback. Special thanks to Ari Berridge, Kim Groves, Candice Brown, Meredith Wilson, and Mellissa Harrison.

Much of my spiritual growth has been influenced by our church pastors, Bart Stone, Seth Hoover, and Luke McGee. I am grateful for the ways they have let God work through them to inspire me and so many others in countless ways.

I am also grateful for the support of our hospital chaplain and author, Gloria Walker, who gave me the book *Pastoral Prayers for the Hospital Visit*; it has been a wonderful help. I have been blessed to work with numerous Christian friends, nurses, and healthcare leaders who have encouraged, inspired, and been a light during difficult situations. I am grateful to have been able to see firsthand what it looks like to be a great Christian leader. Special thanks to Crosslink Publishing for giving life to this creative work inside my heart. My writing career would not be possible without the support of my loving husband, Nick, who still continues to amaze me after all these years. I am forever grateful for our parents who have helped us find Jesus in this life. Above all, I give all honor and thanks to God our Father for His many gifts and blessings and for allowing me to use His gifts for His glory.

CHAPTER 1

Back to Our Roots

If you work in the healthcare profession, there is a great opportunity to spiritually minister to those in need of healing. Sadly, I am not the only healthcare worker who feels weak in this area. Many nurses and healthcare professionals are missing out on this incredible aspect of healing. Recent research confirms that nurses and doctors seldom perform spiritual assessments, the same spiritual assessments that are required by accrediting bodies such as The Joint Commission. (Mamier et al.2017). One common barrier to providing spiritual care is the lack of formal training (Zollfrank et al. 2015). It is true; ask any health care professional if they were taught to pray with their patients in medical or nursing school. The answer is no. We talked about respecting the patient's beliefs, but we weren't taught how to pray. Today, the art of nursing takes place in colleges and universities. While this is a great way to scientifically validate the nursing profession to the rest of the world, there has been a shift in the way we care for our patients. In the university setting, spiritual care might be discussed in a few paragraphs of a leadership book with one or two test questions. However, this was not always the case.

From its origins, nursing care has been holistic in nature (Wynne 2013). In other words, we treated the patient as a whole being, including the mind, the body, and the soul. Pastor Mark Driscoll put it this way, "Cars need gas, lungs need air, and souls need prayer." Twenty-two years earlier, when I was a student in nursing school, a wise older instructor, with translucent silvery hair shared her story of the way nursing school used to be. Her name was Mrs. Paige. I can still see her crystal blue eyes. She went on to explain how back in her day, nursing school took place in a Catholic hospital in the 1950s. She described the old brick hospital dormitories where they slept and how she was trained in the hospital day and night by the Catholic nuns—she interrupted and added with a smile—"who, by the way, did not allow any boyfriends." Unlike today, spiritual care was woven into every aspect of their hands-on training. Somehow along the way we lost this connection. I knew I wanted to connect with my patients on this historically deeper level, but I didn't know how to best utilize this great God given opportunity.

Two months before the great COVID-19 pandemic, I had an incredible opportunity to visit the Florence Nightingale Museum in London. I didn't even know at the time it was the year of Florence Nightingale's 200th Birthday and the Year of the Nurse. Little did I know 2020 would prove to be one of the most challenging years to be a nurse. It was an amazing trip and visiting that small museum was definitely one of many highlights. During her time, Florence herself lived through the Spanish flu pandemic of 1918 and cared for hundreds of flu patients in tents. She introduced basic hygiene principles to the front lines of the First World War. I learned Florence had written hundreds of books and even declined a marriage proposal to pursue her God-given calling to nursing. In one of her notes on nursing, Florence states that caring for the whole patient including the spirit was at the very heart of the principles of nursing. I experienced so much history in London, history of the church and of the nursing profession. I loved how God always had His hand in the church and the church was the very foundation and a pillar for the hospital.

Just like Florence served on the front lines of war during a global flu pandemic, we still battle as nurses and healthcare professionals today. Every day we fight a real battle against an enemy of illness and injury. Sometimes we gain ground, sometimes we lose ground. We fight not with swords or knives, nor with guns or grenades. Instead of swords or knives, we have scalpels and needles. Instead of guns or grenades, we have defibrillators and medicine. The battle is real where life and death hang in the balance. Our weapons are unconventional to war. Our hands are not balled up in fists, but opened to give chest compressions, to help, and to hold. I have spent most of my career perfecting my scientific skills and wielding weapons against illness and injury.

All except one weapon. It is that secret weapon; the one we don't often find in our medical journals or books. It is the hidden weapon we keep on reserve only for when all else fails. We often think of it as the last resort. The funny thing is it doesn't even cost any money. It doesn't require a fancy college degree. Yet even with all the power it contains, we rarely use it. I am talking about the secret weapon of prayer. You know, the one we place in a box on a shelf and only bring out on special occasions if specifically requested by a family member or a patient. It's the weapon you may not be so comfortable wielding. Perhaps it is because we are more comfortable with all our other weapons in the battle against illness and injury. What if you discovered how to use this secret weapon well and weren't afraid of using it? What if we could show others how to use prayer? What if we became confident in its power just as we are in medicine, surgery, and defibrillators?

In Ephesians 6:12, Paul tells us to put on the whole gospel armor as we fight against the spiritual forces of evil and darkness in heavenly places. This gospel armor includes a belt of truth, a breastplate of righteousness, shoes of the gospel of peace, a shield of faith, a helmet of salvation, and the sword of Spirit which is the word of God. Once we have all these armor on, what are we to do? Ephesians 6:18 goes on to say, "**praying** at all times in the Spirit, with all prayer and supplication." Prayer prepares you to march into battle where your character will be tested and developed.

Consider our common historic medical symbol of a snake on a pole which can be found on many of today's medical supplies and businesses. Did you know it originated with Moses over 3,000 years ago before the Romans and Greek gods laid claim to it? In Numbers 21:4, the people began to complain and speak out against God and Moses. Then the Lord sent fiery serpents among the people; they were bitten, and many died. It is believed this "fiery serpent" is none other than the saw-scaled or carpet viper (Biblical Training, 2020).

The saw-scaled viper is orangish-red in color, prefers a rocky terrain like the Arabian Desert, and leaps or "flies" at you like lightning with its painful, deadly bite (Biblical Training, 2020). The bite itself leaves a "fiery" red painful area while the hemotoxic venom causes internal hemorrhaging (Biblical Training, 2020). Then, the people came to Moses and repented. They asked Moses to **pray** to the Lord to take away the serpents.

Sometimes when we pray, we want God to remove the problem so all will be well. However, a good father doesn't always rescue his child from every challenge but instead teaches the child how to work through the problem. I am reminded of the scripture in Psalms 23:4 that states, "Even though I walk *through* the valley of the shadow of death, I will fear no evil, for you are with me; your rod and your staff, they comfort me." Moses prayed and the Lord chose not to remove the fiery serpents. Instead, the Lord made a way through the fiery serpents. He told Moses to make a bronze fiery serpent and set it on a pole, "and everyone who is bitten, when he sees it, shall live." This bronze snake on a pole soon became a symbol of healing to God's people. Some say, in the New Testament, Jesus symbolically took the place of the snake on the pole and by His stripes we are healed.

Many nurses and healthcare professionals openly agree that spiritual care is a very important aspect of healing (Selby et al. 2016). If you've worked in a US hospital you have certainly heard of the accreditation body known as The Joint Commission. But, did you know The Joint Commission even recognizes patients' spiritual needs by requiring hospitals to conduct spiritual assessments (Kelly and Tazbir 2014)? But let us be honest, when was the last time you performed a spiritual assessment on your patient? Or let's flip the question, when is the last time a nurse or doctor performed a spiritual assessment on you as a patient? The closest I have seen is when registration asks if you have a religious preference. Would you consider that a spiritual assessment?

I had been a nurse for 18 years before I learned spiritual distress is an accepted nursing diagnosis according to the North American Nursing Diagnosis Association (NANDA). It means loss of connectivity between life purpose or meaning with self, others, nature, music, art, or greater power (Kelly and Tazbir 2014). Maybe it is just me, but no one I know has ever mentioned it before. When asked to accurately describe spiritual distress, many nurses and healthcare providers honestly do not know how (Selby et al. 2016). If spiritual care is such a vital aspect of patient healing, I wonder what the barriers are to providing this care? What are some simple solutions to providing spiritual care, especially in acute care settings? Could the answer be simply learning how to pray with others so they can hear and see the truth for themselves?

Teaching nurses, doctors, and healthcare professionals to pray with patients comforts our patients on a deeper level while also providing us with more purpose. All over the United States, there are nursing shortages. However, one of the best kept secrets to any job retention and recruitment is connecting employees to their gifts, talents, and purposes. Whether you are a healthcare worker of faith or not, there is no greater joy in this life on earth than finding purpose or being part of a miracle. There is no greater purpose than to bring glory to God while in the service of others. You can't put a price tag on it. It is like that feeling you get when you make a child smile or hug someone you love.

Today, I interviewed a nurse named Beverly who spoke about a time she had to deal with a difficult patient. The patient came to the emergency department (ED) following a seizure. It was change of shift and Beverly had just received the patient report from the off going nurse. Beverly asked the patient, "When was the last time you took your seizure medication?" The patient responded, "What are you, stupid? Didn't you hear the other nurse? I have been off my medication!" The patient went on to call Beverly a few other choice words. Beverly thought about just switching this patient with another nurse since she clearly didn't have a good rapport with her. But instead, she spoke softly and patiently as she went on to describe why she needed to know the last time she took her medication. Somehow, Beverly was able to deescalate the situation. Finally, it was time to discharge the patient. Honestly, Beverly was kind of glad to be sending her home. Then, out of nowhere, the patient grabbed Beverly's hand and asked her, "Will you pray for me?'

Beverly was a little taken aback. Just a few hours ago she was calling Beverly stupid and now, she wanted her to pray for her. But Beverly didn't really feel like she had a choice, the patient literally was holding her by the hand with a pleading look on her face. Not really knowing what to say, Beverly decided to pray for her and somehow the words just came. After she said amen the patient thanked her, and Beverly walked her out the front lobby to go home.

Then without warning the patient gave her a great big goodbye hug in front of all the other patients in the lobby. When the other patients witnessed this hug, in unison the entire waiting room let out an, "Awwww!" Beverly said goodbye, and quickly went back to clean up the patient's room so she could call back the next patient from the waiting room. When she called on the next patient, the next patient confessed she had just been praying to get a nurse like Beverly and now she had! It made me wonder how many times does just being in the hospital cause a person to pray and seek God? By the end of the interview, Beverly was in tears and so was I. Beverly said, "It just made me feel so good to be able to help her on such an unexpected deeper level."

Another nursing colleague, Paula, shared how she was in triage one day when another nurse named Susan called her over to help with her patient, a young mother who was in tears. The patient had signed in with a headache. Susan went on to explain what had happened. The patient was having a headache but was also spiritually and emotionally distressed. You see, she was the mother of two small children and out of the kindness of her own heart had taken in her friend's older child, a 13-year-old boy. His mother was going through some hard times and this mother offered to help.

This mother had recently discovered some shocking videos on this child's phone that unveiled a horrifying truth. This truth wounded her to her very core causing her immense physical, spiritual, and emotional pain. She found videos of this 13-year-old boy sexually abusing her own two smaller children. Paula and Susan's heart instantly broke for this young mother. Sure, they could offer her medicine for her headache, but the source of her pain was so much deeper than the physical. Then, Susan asked the patient if she and Paula could pray for her. She agreed, and Paula and Susan gently laid hands on her and began to pray for her. Paula doesn't remember all that was said during the prayer, but as they prayed, she said, "You could just feel the warmth as the weight and heaviness of the situation lifted off of this mother." Afterwards, this mom looked and felt more at peace and surprisingly, so did Paula and Susan. Paula went on to say, "Often, I don't think we consider that the physical, spiritual, and mental being are so intertwined they can have powerful effects on us physically."

I recently discovered how praying could even be useful in improving customer service. If you work in a hospital, or any business, customer service scores are frequently tied to financial reimbursement. As a nurse, provider, or technician we may be in the healthcare business, but truly we are in the business of caring for people. Last week, I was passing through radiology on my way back to my office and I noticed a man in a wheelchair in the hallway. He looked stressed, but I saw that he was being cared for by the radiology technician. I went to my office and needed some supplies for my next class, so I headed back the way I had come. He was still waiting there and this time he was angry asking me if I knew where his technician had gone and why was it taking him so long to go back to his room. I said, "I don't know, let me check." Another radiology technician saw me and said he was waiting on the transporter to take him back. I asked if it would be okay for me to take him back instead. She agreed, handed me his chart, and then her eyes got big as she mouthed the words "THANK YOU, "so that the patient could not hear or see her. I supposed that meant this patient had already proven to be quite a handful. I gave a nod and set off to wheel this patient back to his room. He complained the entire way back to his room. Things were certainly not going as planned for him. He was supposed to go home, but then he had a terrible headache, and now the doctor wanted an MRI of his brain. He had his MRI but was still in terrible pain. No one had fixed his pain, he couldn't go home, and this hospital stay was costing him money. I've been told I am a good listener, so I used my gift of listening and just let him vent the whole way back.

As we approached his room, I promised I would speak to his nurse and address his concerns with her. He didn't seem satisfied with that response, stating, "I already told her, and she didn't do anything." So, I thought I would try something different. I remembered something Pastor Mark

Driscoll had said, "When there is nothing else you can do, there is always one thing you can do."

I asked him if I could pray for him. He looked at me a little surprised and, protecting his pride, he said, "Well, if it would make you feel better, you can pray with me." Seeing there was not much else I could offer, I decided to give it a try. I helped him back into bed and prayed over him. I thanked God, that health and wholeness was being restored into him, his pain was easing, and that the peace and comfort that surpasses all understanding was washing over him. It was a simple prayer from the heart. As we prayed, surprisingly his demeanor changed. He even smiled and thanked me. His nurse arrived just as I was leaving, so I updated her about his concerns and asked if he could have something for pain. She thanked me and I headed to gather my supplies. I never saw him again, so I'll never know if the prayer worked. However, I do know that I did everything I could, and he knew I really cared. Isn't this why many of us love working in healthcare, to truly care for people? It made me wonder if we could improve our service recovery scores by simply adding prayer to our process improvement plans.

As Pastor Bart Stone once said, "Are you connecting with your purpose? Are we laboring in faith on purpose from a position of joy." -One of my favorite quotes by Marc Anthony is "If you love what you do, you'll never have to work another day in your life." Matthew 5: 14–16 says, "You are the light of the world. A city set on a hill cannot be hidden. Nor do people light a lamp and put it under a basket, but stand, and it gives light to all in the house. In the same way, let your light shine before others, so that they may see your good works and give glory to your Father who is in heaven."

Every year, my children are assigned a service ministry project. In this project, they have to think of a way to serve others in the community and show Jesus to others. This particular year, prior to the pandemic of 2020, they decided they wanted to go to the hospital and pray with anyone who wanted prayer. So, we set a date and time and I got permission from our executive vice president at the hospital. Over Thanksgiving break, we got up and got dressed and headed to the hospital. We arrived at the hospital at 9 a.m. and started in the hospital chapel. There I laid out the rules and objectives of the day. Then, we prayed for God's Holy Spirit to be present with us and to bless our work, the hospital, and all the patients and staff. I guided my kids through the hospital as we proceeded to check in with nurses on every unit to see if anyone wanted us to pray with them or if they had any patients who might want to be prayed for. Maybe it's just because we live in the south, but surprisingly we were welcomed on every unit. No one turned us away.

One patient, who we will call Lisa, tearfully confessed that our arrival to pray with her was God's perfect timing. She had a chronic medical condition that was causing her pain and suffering. She longed to be able to go home and be with her daughter. We held hands and prayed for her health to be restored and my 12-year-old son prayed for her to be well enough to go home and play with her daughter, my 15-year-old daughter prayed for peace, comfort, ease of pain and sealed it with an amen. I could not have been prouder of our two children than in that very moment. Then, something unexpected happened. Lisa was so moved by our prayer that she wanted to pray for us. We were kind of caught off guard; we really weren't expecting anything in return from anyone. Lisa prayed a beautiful blessing over my children and me. By the end, we were both full of tears. I had never met Lisa until that day, but because of the beautiful connection we shared in prayer, I will never forget her.

We visited every unit. Some areas' staff wanted us to pray with them. In other units, staff and patients wanted us to pray with them. Even in areas that are restricted, such as the operating room, we decided to stand outside the entrance and pray a blessing over that team and its patients.

With permission, we visited the ICU. Now, maybe it is different in other regions and hospitals, but in my experience, there is sort of an unspoken rivalry between the ICU and ED teams. The ICU team gives the ED a hard time and the ED staff give it back in the most petty and passive aggressive ways possible. I work to mend these relationships whenever possible, but culture can be so hard to change. I really wished we had a better relationship between our teams. However, today was different. My kids and I were accepted to the ICU with wide open arms. The ICU charge nurse informed us about a conscious patient who might want prayer. She was a beautiful old soul who we will call Betty.

Betty was diagnosed with metastatic liver cancer. I could tell by the look on the ICU nurses' face that her prognosis was not good. We washed our hands and introduced ourselves to Betty and asked her and her son if she would like us to pray with her. She smiled and welcomed us to pray with her. I saw her son sitting off to the side, so I invited him too. With a single tear rolling down his cheek, he joined in our small prayer circle.

We asked God to be with her and to restore health and wholeness into her and fill her with peace and comfort, my son asked for her to be well for Thanksgiving so she could be with her family and friends again. While I prayed these things, I had this feeling that God was going to restore her health, but I also had this feeling that God was going to call her home soon. After we sealed our prayer with "in Jesus's holy and precious name, Amen," I think. Betty felt it too. Afterwards, she smiled warmly and said, "However God chooses to heal me, on Earth or in Heaven, I know He will do it." Then Betty looked over at my daughter, Brooklynn, and said, "Now, I can tell you are a cool girl." Then she looked at my son and said, "But this one, I can tell, he is humble." It is so indescribably beautiful how we could connect and show true selfless love and compassion for a total stranger in need within a matter of minutes just by praying with them. At this point, Betty's son had tears streaming down both of his cheeks, which caused me to start welling up with tears. Betty and her son thanked us for praying with them and we thanked them for letting us pray with them. It is hard to describe in words the closeness and love that you can experience through praying with others.

After we left Betty, we went back to the ICU nurses' station to see if they wanted us to pray with anyone else. The ICU manager and about five other ICU nurses decided they all wanted to pray with us for their department and for each other. We formed a small circle right there in the ICU nurses' station and prayed many blessings over the ICU team and for each other. Then something strange and unexpected happened. For the first time ever, the whole ICU team looked at me differently. They no longer saw a representative of their long-time archnemesis and rival ED team. It was as if I was now one of them, welcomed into their inner circle of trust. I had, on some level, always felt a little bit unwelcome to the ICU at multiple hospitals. But after the prayer, I felt it, pure selfless compassion for one another. I thought to myself, "Wow, maybe I should have done this years ago!"

In all, we spent about three hours of our day praying with people in every unit of the hospital. Some were colleagues and some were patients. I have to say, there is something peculiar about volunteering to serve others. You get up and get dressed with full intentions to go and help others. However, when you finish you realize they helped you on a deeper unexpected level that you did not even know you needed. We left feeling like a void had been filled in our hearts that we did not know existed. It was a blessing to partake in my kid's service ministry project because afterwards, I felt more confident in praying with others and so did my children.

I realize that service and healthcare jobs can be very difficult emotionally, spiritually, and physically. But as children of God, it is not really us doing any of the work. We know that we can do all things through Him who strengthens us (Philippians 4:13). Maybe, if we connected back to our roots and our purpose, and drew from His strength instead of our own, we could bring forth God's forgiveness and healing to those in need.

Right in front of us on a daily basis we have this incredible access to people to show them God's love, mercy, and healing. For years, I never considered that the greatest risk for the Kingdom of God may not be something I did or read, but a conversation I had about prayer. Are you happy with your healthcare career? Are you connecting your life purpose with the work you have right in front of you? A wise lady who found Jesus while lying in a hospital bed, once said, "Let your mission field be the ground right between your own two feet." In other words, you don't have to travel across the world on a mission trip to be a healing light to someone in need right in front of you. Have you ever met a human being that did not want to be loved, encouraged, forgiven, inspired, or healed? Are we keeping God's powerful good news to ourselves? "The kingdom of God belongs to risk takers, not comfort seekers or people pleasers," - Pastor Bart Stone. Another one of my favorite quotes is, "Life begins at the end of your comfort zone," by Neale Donald Walsch. If you have ever worked in a critical care area, you know all too well that life is so very fragile and short that every day really is a gift. So, I write this to encourage others of faith: "Don't let your light be hidden under a basket." After healing many, Jesus says in Matthew 9:37"The harvest is plentiful, but the laborers are few."

Discussion Questions

1. Has a patient or a sick loved one ever asked you to pray with them?

2. Have you ever asked a patient if they would like you to pray with them?

3. What do you think it means to perform a spiritual assessment on someone?

Pray that God will open your heart and mind and teach you how to make prayer a part of your daily patient care.

Prayer Example
Faithful God, here and now, we openly welcome your Holy Spirit into our hearts and minds. We seek your wisdom, reveal to us how to make prayer a part of our daily patient care. Help us to truly comfort and connect with our patients on a deeper spiritual level. We thank you for your provision, protection, mercy, and grace. Cleanse us of our sins and help us to be a light for others to see your Glory in the people you set before us Lord. We ask you to bless us to help bring forth healing and restore wholeness throughout the day. In your holy, precious, and powerful name, we pray. Amen.

CHAPTER 2

Expect the Unexpected

Sometimes what our Father has in store for us is so much bigger than what we could ever expect or imagine. I remember the first time I ever witnessed a miracle on the job. I was in my mid-twenties working in a busy suburban emergency room (ER) in Georgia. I can still hear the cries of this patient's wife pleading with God for her husband's life. My colleagues were performing cardiopulmonary resuscitation (CPR) on a middle-aged man in Room 1. He had come in by ambulance in full cardiac arrest and his wife arrived just minutes later. The code team was running through the advanced cardiac life support algorithms like clockwork. The truth is real emergency nursing was never like in TV shows. In my own personal experience, it was very seldom that we ever see people survive death, even despite our calculated resuscitative efforts. To be completely honest, at this moment, I did not have high expectations for this poor lady's husband.

I was walking down the hallway towards Room 1. His wife was told to stand outside the doorway with our secretary, Becky, but she could see her husband receiving CPR through the glass door. Right there in the middle of the hallway, his wife got down on her knees and with all of her breath and all her might, pleaded out loud with God. The way she was yelling so loudly, she could be heard by every person in the entire ED, including everyone in the waiting room! I had never witnessed anyone cry out to God with such passion and desire. My heart sank as did those of everyone who could hear her pleas. People from every direction stopped what they were doing and were just staring at her.

I dug deep into courage and walked towards her to console her. All my past nursing experience had proven time and time again that people do not often come back to life. How was I going to make her understand her husband was dead? As tears started to well up in my eyes and a small lump formed in my throat, I placed my hand softly on her shoulder. To be honest, I don't think she even noticed me. She just kept begging God not to take her husband. "PLEASE, GOD, PLEASE. NOT

NOW, GOD. DON'T TAKE HIM, PLEASE, GOD, NO!" Then, we heard the doctor say through the glass door, "Wait, is that a pulse?", followed by a chuckle of disbelief. "YES, we have a pulse. We have a pulse!" She jumped up to look at her husband. Then she started shouting praises, "THANK YOU, LORD! OH THANK YOU, LORD! THANK YOU, JESUS!"

What? I was just as shocked and surprised as everyone else. At that moment, I realized that it was her prayers that saved her husband that day. Everyone present witnessed this miracle and were so incredibly happy for her. As a young Christian nurse, it was by far the greatest moment I had ever bore witness to at the time in my career. Seeing God's response to the lady's prayer, reaffirmed my own faith. But sadly, that is where it seemingly ended that day. No one ever asked how this miracle happened, or should we pray more often with our patients or loved ones? The truth is, some prayers work and others do not. Have you ever wondered why? Are there certain qualities that cause one prayer to work better than others? If there are ways to improve our communication with each other, is there a way to improve our communication with and understanding of God?

In hindsight, her prayers had certain qualities. In Psalms 9:1 it says, "I will praise you, Oh Lord with all my heart." She looked up and shouted to the Lord with her whole heart boldly and fear-lessly. Even though most of the medical team did not have high expectations, it did not stop her. I realize now what great faith it must have taken to expect the unexpected. That is what faith is all about anyway, isn't it? In James 5:15, it says, "And the prayer of faith will save the one who is sick, and the Lord will raise him up. And if he has committed sins, he will be forgiven." Nevertheless, it would be more than a decade before I connected how I could foster such faith-filled prayers as a nurse and a patient.

Along my prayer journey, I was learning more and more. I don't know why, but sometimes I forget to ask for God's help with the small things too. Maybe I think I am supposed to be able to fix the little things myself. For instance, my two little picky eaters. Well, they are not so little anymore, but I have spent all kinds of energy, money, and time trying to get my kids to eat a greater variety of foods. We have tried rewards, games, cooking together, making new recipes, visiting nutrition-ists, nutrition apps, special plates, and we even saw a psychologist. We would make a little prog-ress, but not much. Well, after all these measures and efforts, I just felt like I was never going to get them to eat better. However, as I was learn-ing about prayer, I realized this was not too big or small for my heavenly Father. At this point, I had run out of ideas. The only thing left I could think of doing was to give it to God, after all He can do what man can't. So that is exactly what I did.

I thanked Him that He was causing my children to want to eat better and try new foods. I reminded myself that it was God's will for my children to grow up to be healthy and whole so they could be all that He created them to be. I prayed about this every morning when I woke up. Then, after only about a week, the craziest things started happening. God did in a week what I could not do in a decade. I knew it was possible, and prayed with expectancy, but I still could not help but be so impressed. God really exceeded my expectations. All of the sudden, without prompting, my son wanted to grill up a steak dinner and my daughter wanted to have a chicken sandwich. These were both foods my kids have never eaten. They were both trying new foods at school and encouraging the other to try what they had tried. Wait a minute, you mean all this time, all I had to do was pray to God? I really wish someone would have told me that about ten years ago. But I am really glad I finally asked. I guess, it is never too late. God is good at helping with the little things just as He is with the big, crazy, and unexpected things.

During an unexpected admission to the hospital, God revealed to me another surprising truth about prayer and healing. In May of 2020, as the

COVID-19- pandemic started to wind down a little, I awoke at 3 a.m. with pressure in my stomach and nausea. I'm part-Japanese; we historically fix everything with hot tea. I was sure a little ginger mint and fennel tea would do the trick and calm my stomach right down. I got up and heated up a cup and drank small slow sips. I did feel a little better and went back to sleep. I awoke to my alarm clock and got ready for work. My stomach was still a little aggravated and I did not have an appetite. I decided I would drink another cup of tea on the way to work and all would be well. That morning, I was teaching our ED Orientation class on-line via Zoom. I didn't feel any better, but it was tolerable. I did not have any appetite, so I skipped breakfast. Soon it was time for lunch, and nothing looked appealing in the cafeteria. I decided to eat a cup of dry Cheerios, thinking surely that it would be a safe bet. Eating the Cheerios actually felt good. After lunch, I went back to my computer and started reviewing documentation on Zoom with our new employees. I got about 45 minutes into the lesson and then the nausea became overwhelming. I excused myself and called my colleague, Natasha, to see if she could take over.

She arrived and took over my Zoom lecture within 5 minutes. I made my way to the bathroom. I thought, maybe if I just would vomit, I would feel better. The only problem was I didn't have to throw up. The color in my face had turned about 10 shades of pale and I was hyperventilating. A colleague stopped me in the hall and asked if I was okay; I lied and said I was okay. I thought to myself, if I can just go and lie down, I will feel so much better. I don't even know how I managed but, somehow, I was able to drive myself home. When I pulled into the garage, I felt so bad, I called my husband and told him to come help me out of the car. At first, he must have thought I was gravely injured in a car accident by the sound of my voice. He promptly helped me to the bathroom. He agreed, I looked like I was about to vomit. Yet again, nothing happened. I reluctantly was directed to lie down on my bed and my son came to check my temperature. I didn't have a fever. "At least it's not COVID-19," I thought to myself, this must be some awful stomach bug.

No matter which way I laid, I could not escape the discomfort. It wasn't till I realized I was still hyperventilating that I thought to myself this is not okay. Shortly afterwards, my husband came back to check on me and directed me to see a doctor. Now, even when there wasn't a COVID-19- pandemic, I never wanted to visit a doctor. I realized that sounds a little strange coming from a nurse, but as they say, us nurses are the worst patients and I fit the stereotype perfectly. I hesitated and then gave him the okay to call the advice line to verify the COVID-19- procedure for emergencies. He asked me what it felt like. I said, "Remember the movie *Aliens*? Well, it feels like one of those aliens is going to burst through and come right out of my stomach." With a half-smile, he understood the seriousness of my condition.

We put on our masks and he drove me to the hospital. On the way over I prayed, "Lord, please give me good nurses and doctors and bless them with wisdom, compassion, strength, and kindness." The door greeter checked our temperatures and screened us for COVID-19 as we entered the building; I was placed in a wheelchair. My husband was allowed to wheel me to check me in. I was given an armband. Nick moved me to the waiting room, where he prayed over me and then he was asked to wait in the car. It was so strange not having him with me. There were only two other patients in the waiting room with me. All of a sudden I felt a little lonely. I closed my eyes and reminded God, that He said he would never leave me nor forsake me. Then, I remembered that though this was a surprise to me, it was not a surprise to Him and that He was still in control. Soon a nurse came around the corner and called, "Jennifer!? Jennifer is that you?" It was as if she was unsure whether she knew me from somewhere. Although she was wearing a mask and I could only see her eyes, I recognized her. I said, "Is that you, Debbie?" Debbie and I had worked together a few years back. I knew right then God had given me a great nurse, and everything was going to be okay.

Debbie triaged me with her calming yet concerned way about her. After triage, I now had a room and eagerly waited to see a doctor. All I knew was I was nauseated and there was an enormous amount of pressure on the right side of my stomach. So much that it radiated all the way up to my right shoulder. It wasn't till the doctor examined me and palpated the lower right side of my abdomen that I recognized the source of the pain. Still, I told myself it was probably just really bad gas and maybe everything was going to be okay. Afterward, she ordered a CT scan of my abdomen, blood work, antibiotics, pain medication, nausea medication, and IV fluids. Now, as a nurse, I had administered Toradol and Zofran for pain and nausea to my patients thousands of times, but I had never received them. I am here to tell you they were wonderful medications. I felt ten times better!

While I sat awaiting my CT results, I knew what could be wrong, but I didn't want to jump to any conclusions until we were sure. Thoughts ran through my mind like this only happens to other people and, statistically, only to young men.

Maybe she will come back and just tell me I have a really bad stomach virus. I thanked the Lord for FaceTime. At least I could see my husband and my parents and let them know what was going on. I told him it was going to be a while and he should go get something to eat and check on the kids.

He reluctantly agreed and I promised to call as soon as I found out anything. Hours went by before the doctor came back to my room and told me what I didn't want to hear, "Well, it looks like you have appendicitis." Half of me knew it and the other half was in disbelief. It felt surreal. I asked her what was next? She said she needed to call a surgeon, but I would most likely be transferred to a hospital downtown. I asked if my husband could take me and stay with me in that hospital, she gave me a frown and said unfortunately no, but we will arrange our own transportation and take you there. I frowned and tried to face the reality of the ticking time bomb in my abdomen. She said she would return after she spoke with the surgeon.

I told my husband, and he gathered some things to take with me to the hospital. We messaged our friends, family, and life group from church to pray that I would get a good surgeon and to pray for the doctors, nurses, and healthcare workers taking care of me. Nick brought me a phone charger, change of clothes, and toiletries. I gave him my purse and wedding band as I knew they would ask me to take off everything for surgery. Then, he was asked to leave again. I felt so alone, helpless, and vulnerable.

I fell asleep for a little while, only to awake and find out emergency medical services (EMS) was delayed for 2 more hours. I had not ever ridden in the back of an ambulance as a patient. It felt so weird and humbling being on this side of the stretcher. Finally, they arrived, buckled me up in their stretcher, and our bumpy adventure downtown began. We entered the downtown hospital through a back-parking deck in the middle of the night and followed a labyrinth of hallways up to my hospital room. It had been eleven years since I had worked at the ED here. Some parts of the hospital looked familiar and others unrecognizable. I looked at the clock; it was 2 a.m.. The nurse and tech arrived to check me in. The EMT said good-bye and wished me well as a new armband was placed on my wrist.

I asked when my surgery was going to take place and the nurse said the COVID-19 team would have to test me for COVID-19 before we could schedule it. "Oh, okay," I said, "when will they do that?" She answered, "It won't be until the morning; they only come on day shift." I decided to grab my phone and email a nurse mentor and dearest friend of mine who worked at the hospital, just to let her know I was here if she had time to swing by and say hi. Paula got my email when she came into work that morning and came to see me.

Seeing her that morning gave me such a great comfort in the absence of my husband. Not only did she come and say hi, but she had also stopped by the gift shop and bought me a little smiley face mug, a balloon, my favorite lip gloss, and lovely smelling toiletries. She was so incredibly thoughtful and supportive. She sat down and visited for a bit. It was 9:30 now and I still didn't have a COVID-19 test. To top that off, the doctor said it could take 6–14 hours for the results because they were no longer doing rapid tests. At this point, it had been 30 hours since I started to feel bad and looked like I would have to wait a lot longer. The pain was becoming incredible. Paula asked, "Do you want me to ask the nurse if I can collect your COVID-19 swab?" Paula was most certainly qualified. After all, Paula had just finished training about a hundred ER nurses how to collect a proper COVID-19 sample. I agreed, and she was granted permission. She collected my COVID-19 swab deep inside my left nostril till my left eye started to tear up. It really wasn't as bad as I had originally thought it might be. With a few twists she took out the swab and labeled it. Then she walked it to the lab herself. Now, I don't know who she talked to down there or what she did, but my COVID-19 test results were back in 4 hours! Thankfully, the test was negative. I thanked God; He had sent me another guardian angel in the form of a nurse.

I was in too much pain to consider it at the time. But in hindsight, it dawned on me that maybe as a nurse, I too had been a guardian angel to hundreds of people and never fully understood the impact of my role. Maybe my patients and their families were praying to God to place a nurse such as myself at the right place and time. After Paula had gone back to work, I struggled to get some rest and updated my family as to what was happening. The doctor came back to explain we were just waiting for a time slot in the operating room (OR) now and that either he or his partner would perform the procedure. They had given me morphine about 10 hours before and offered me more, but I really hated the way it made me feel. I requested Toradol instead, but I couldn't have any more because it causes bleeding, and we were too close to surgery. I thought for sure I could handle this situation without extra medicine and surgery was just around the corner. The pressure came back with a vengeance! My feet started to feel tingly. I had this uncontrollable urge to stand up and pace. Then the nausea and hyperventilating came back, overwhelming me. Something was rapidly happening and physically changing in me.

I called my nurse, and she gave me more nausea medication, but it didn't help this time. I didn't realize the severe pain was causing the nausea. It was about 6 p.m. and Paula had gotten off work and came to check on me again, right after I vomited in the bathroom. I was clammy and pale. At this moment, I felt like I had no control over anything, and my life was literally in God's hands. I was completely dependent on Him. Paula consoled me like a mother hen and sat with me. I told her she didn't have to stay after work, but she insisted, and I was too weak to argue.

In this moment of complete dependence on God, I prayed. In my prayers, I thanked God He was lining up the right surgeon at exactly the right moment, and that He was in complete control of the situation even though I was not. I was learning to pray with expectancy in the midst of the storm when all felt lost and was spiraling out of control. I didn't know why this was happening to me, but somewhere deep down inside I knew that all of this suffering was for a reason. I kept reminding myself that this was not a surprise to God and that He has me in the palm of His hand.

I was praying and pacing. It felt like my ticking time bomb was going to burst at any moment. Paula went to ask and see if they had a time slot in surgery for me. The nurse came back with good news. I had a surgery time, and it was time to start preparing for surgery with a chlorhexidine bed bath. On that note, Paula left to give me some privacy. There was hope on the horizon! After I was all cleaned up, I was just waiting for a transporter to come and get me. I had never been so glad to see a hospital transporter in my life! At that point, I was willing to give him a scalpel and let him cut it out himself. In my excitement, I almost forgot that I promised to tell my husband when I was going into surgery. I quickly texted my family to let them know I was going into surgery now.

When I got down to the OR, the nurses checked me in, took my vital signs, and asked me questions. I was in so much pain at that point; I would say it was equal or worse than childbirth. I was still hyperventilating and squirming around in bed from the severe pressure inside my abdomen. The surgeon was not the same doctor I met earlier that day; she introduced herself as his medical partner. I reminded myself, she is the right surgeon at the right time. She took one look at me and said, "Let's give her some fentanyl. Normally, I detest taking narcotic pain medication, but at this point I would have taken anything. The doctor gave me a concerned look and said if my appendix had already ruptured then the scar would be much bigger. However, if it has not ruptured yet then I would just have 3 small scars that would hardly be noticeable, and I could even wear a bikini. Honestly, I could care less about the bikini and would have let her cut me all the way across at that point.

That was the last thing I remember. Suddenly I woke up to another guardian angel nurse calling my name. I was back in my hospital room. Six hours later it was 1:00 a.m. I can't even remember how I got there. I felt so drowsy. The nurse, Bethany, introduced herself as the night shift charge nurse and caught me up to speed on what had happened. I shifted in the bed to try and sit up. I was sore, but that excruciating pressure pain was gone! Praise Jesus! I could tolerate a little soreness. I learned the OR team had caught it just before it ruptured. Bethany and I examined the scars together and I only had the three small incisions covered in skin glue, so I could even shower later! I really did get the right surgeon at the right time. She was actually just beginning her shift when I came down to the OR; the other doctor I met had gone home for the day. The nurse said it was time for my pain medication and I decided I would be a good patient and listen this time. I took a deep breath and knew everything was going to be okay. I was learning to pray with expectancy and my faith was growing. Around 2:00 a.m. I was having a hard time falling back to sleep, so I turned on the TV and the first thing I saw was a familiar pastor teaching about faith. It gave me great comfort, and at some point, I drifted off to sleep again.

Looking back, I think the hardest part is having faith and trusting when everything is falling apart. When all is lost and hopeless, self-reliance is no longer an option. I learned about humility, dependence on God, and gained a whole other perspective of what it feels like to be a patient with no family present to help. All I had was God, healthcare workers, prayers, and expectations that all was going to be well. I think it is important to understand that as healthcare workers, we play a significant role not just in healing but in a person's spiritual walk with God. How many times does God use us to bring hope, comfort, and peace to so many people and we think we are just doing our job? In hindsight, this experience taught me three things. It grew my faith, by testing me through suffering. It taught me what it feels like to be a patient without any family at my bedside. Lastly, it taught me what my role as a nurse might mean to my patients.

As I was writing this book, Niki, a mom from my kid's school, shared with me how the whole OR team unexpectedly gave her hope, peace, and comfort just before her son's surgery. See, her son, who at the time was a high school senior, has rare multiple congenital heart defects. For one, his heart is located on the right side of his chest and he may have to eventually receive an adult heart transplant. Most people with this condition don't make it beyond young adulthood without a successful heart transplant. She explained how he has had multiple heart surgeries since birth. At the children's hospital, it was common practice to call the parents back to see their child just before they begin surgery. Niki came in to see her son and then the doctor and the whole OR team paused and prayed out loud over her son, and for each other. Niki didn't expect them to do that, but it gave her such deep comfort and relief. As tears streamed down her face, a peace that surpassed all understanding washed over her. She knew God was right there with her son even when she couldn't be. If we prayed more often, I wonder how many others would be comforted and feel God's presence in the middle of life's storms.

Discussion Questions

1. Has God ever exceeded your expectations?

2. Have you ever found yourself helpless in the middle of one of life's storms? What did you do? Who did you turn to?

3. What are some of God's promises to us in the Bible? Are you expecting those promises to occur in your own life? Read Psalm 91.

Ask God to help you to pray with more expectancy. Remind God of some of His promises. Thank God that He is in control and the things that may be unexpected to us are no surprise to Him.

Prayer Example
Practice writing your own prayer example below.

_____

_____

_____

_____

_____

_____

Chapter 3

When God Heals Instantly

As an ER nurse of 19 years at the time, I had become well-skilled in the art of accurately caring for the ill or injured body and mind, but still shied away from caring for spiritual needs. I hadn't experienced first-hand how spiritual care could foster stronger patient-caregiver relationships, provide hope, and offer better coping mechanisms in the presence of illness (Zollfrank et al. 2015). Perhaps, it is the chaotic environment of the ER or because I never received formal spiritual care training. Maybe it's because I felt uncomfortable praying out loud, or maybe I just did not want to offend anyone. I guess, in a way, I have always been a bit of a people pleaser and a rule follower. I have usually done what I was told. Then one day a dear friend and colleague of mine, Shunda Harper, shared some biblical teaching from Galatians 1:10 that posed the question, "Do I want the praise of man or God?" The verse goes like this, "For am I now seeking the approval of man, or of God? Or am I trying to please man? If I were still trying to please man, I would not be a servant of Christ." It spoke to me so much that even today it still sits in my office as a reminder. I have always longed to be bold and fearless in my faith and walk with Christ, but I sincerely struggle with what others might think of me if I did. Has this ever happened to you?

Then one day I realized I had been missing out on something indescribably powerful. The opportunity came in the midst of tragedy. I was the family presence nurse for an 18-year-old girl in full cardiac arrest. This was an emotionally difficult assignment. I stayed with the family during the code and kept them informed of what was happening to their daughter. She, a young senior high school student with her whole life ahead of her, suddenly collapsed while getting ready for school one morning. She had no past medical history or signs of overdose. Her mom happened to be going to work late that day when she heard a loud crashing sound in the upstairs bathroom. She rushed up the stairs and yelled through the door, "What happened, are you okay?" There was no response, she swung open the bathroom door to find her daughter unresponsive on the floor. She could hear her own heart pounding through her chest as she reached for her daughter's cell phone by the sink to dial 911. The 911 dispatcher instructed her to put the phone on speaker mode as they instructed the mom on how to perform CPR on her own daughter.

In the ER private family room, I held the mother's hand and asked if she wanted to be present in her daughter's room while we tried to resuscitate her. I tried to explain the horrific scene she was about to witness, a scene no mother should ever have to see. She agreed, and with my arm around her we pushed open the double doors to the trauma room to experience every mother's worst nightmare. I gave her a chair to sit in as I explained what was happening to her daughter. She looked at me through tears of devastation streaming down her cheeks. Then from one mother to another, I could not help but want to offer her something more, more than just evidenced-based practice, more than science, and more than medicine.

Then I felt it, the Holy Spirit, it was more like a tugging gut feeling rather than an audible voice. Try as I might, I couldn't ignore it. They say true courage means moving ahead despite the fear. So, I mustered up what courage I had and asked the one question that made me uncomfortable, "Do you want me to pray with you?" Part of me hoped she would just say, no thank you. To my surprise, she desperately pleaded for me to pray with her. I didn't tell her that I wasn't any good at praying or had little to no experience praying during a cardiac arrest. At the moment, I kind of forgot about that. Despite what the media says, when it comes right down to life and death, the truth is a lot of patients want to be cared for spiritually (Zollfrank et al. 2015). In fact, 74.9% of Americans confess to believing in God or a higher power (Zollfrank et al. 2015). I hadn't really had any time to think this through; I didn't even know what I was going to say. Although praying out loud was not one of my strengths, I had recently read an encouraging book entitled, *The Battle Plan for Prayer* by Stephen and Alex Kindrex. As I prayed, the words surprisingly just flowed out of my mouth. The Lord provided the words, all I had to do was trust and be obedient. I don't remember everything I said, but I do remember asking for God's Holy Spirit to be present and to bless everyone in the room working on her daughter. I asked for healing for her daughter and comfort and peace for the mother. It was a simple prayer from the heart.

But after we prayed, things didn't get better. I began to wonder how I was going to tell that poor mother that it did not look promising despite the code team's efforts and our prayers. Later, her niece arrived to comfort her and wanted to pray again. So, the three of us strangers held hands and prayed again. This reminded me of the scripture in Matthew 18:19–20, "Again I say to you, if two of you agree on earth about anything they ask, it will be done for them by my Father in heaven. For where two or three are gathered in my name, there am I among them." By this point we had been working on her daughter for nearly an hour and had gone through almost all of the Advanced Cardiac Life Support (ACLS) algorithms without any improvement. I knew soon the doctor would have to consider calling the code to an end, sealing it with a time of death. But just as all seemed lost, at the next pulse check, behold! She had a pulse!

As tears of mourning transformed to tears of joy, there was no denying this pulse was nothing short of a miracle! Everyone on the code team was in disbelief. While we had a pulse, we were nowhere near out of the woods yet. The team was now placing her on the ventilator and hanging IV drips. I stood explaining what was happening to the mother.

Now, I've always been told that hearing is the last of the five senses to go, so always be mindful of what you say in front of an unconscious patient. Afterwards, I placed the mother at her daughter's bedside and told her that her daughter, though unresponsive, may still be able to hear her. I told her, "This is your opportunity, if there is anything you want to say to her, give her words of encouragement." I still can't explain it, but it was as if the faith of every person in that room was restored in that moment. To this day, my colleagues still remember her. Before I prayed, I was afraid, but afterward, there was this peace that came over me. Then our medical director, who was leading the code team, admitted that he too was praying. I didn't even know he was a Christian. Suddenly, I realized I had been missing out on one of the most beautiful, powerful, and compassionate aspects of healing, prayer. A few weeks later, it made me smile to see a couple of other nurses randomly praying with their own patients. My confidence in prayer was growing. As a leader you learn that courage and fear are both contagious. I wondered if my courage and obedience in prayer gave others the encouragement they needed to pray with their patients too?

When my friend Meredith heard about this story of healing, she said she too had experienced instant healing before. She had found herself lying in the dark trying to survive the second day of a terrible migraine. Due to COVID-19-, all three of her children were home with her and her husband had gone to work. She had already taken the day off work and she wanted nothing more than to just play with her kids. However, this migraine had her completely out of commission. She had resorted to turning on the TV for her kids and went back to lie down with the lights out. While just lying there in bed with her eyes closed, she decided she wanted to listen to something. She reached for her phone and found the Joyce Meyer app. She honestly never really used this app but decided to click on it and listen to one of Joyce's sermons.

The message was very encouraging. Afterwards, Joyce was praying for healing. She mentioned, "By Jesus's stripes we are healed." From the violent act of people actually whipping Jesus, we are healed. Meredith remembers she had heard of others saying that before and recalls the scripture from Isaiah 53:5. It states, "But he was wounded for our transgressions; he was bruised for our iniquities; the chastisement of our peace was upon him, and with His stripes we are healed." However, Meredith had never really given it much thought before. Afterwards, it was like a light bulb turned on inside her, she thought to herself, "Oh through Jesus's stripes comes healing." Meredith decided that day, when she heard it, she was going to believe it. She just thought of it and decided she was just going to simply believe and that was it. It seemed so simple; in the past she thought of faith as something else. She never knew she could just proclaim and believe it. She always thought that faith was something she had to do inside and change something within her. But all of a sudden, it was as simple as just deciding it was true and believing it was true. Meredith said she decided there really was healing in His stripes.

Joyce Meyers went on to pray for healing for all sorts of different types of serious illnesses. She prayed for the healing of cancer, depression, and a long list of medical conditions. While Meredith lay there listening, she was almost just waiting for it. Meredith said, "I just knew she is going to say migraines, and I am going to be healed." Then at the very end, almost randomly, Joyce added "and migraines." Then Meredith prayed, "God I believe that through your Son's stripes, I am going to be healed and that is it. Amen."

Then instantly the migraine was gone; Meredith felt better! She got up and was almost in disbelief of what had just happened. She thought to herself, is this some sort of mind game, am I going to feel terrible again in a few minutes? But surprisingly she continued to feel better. Through her belief and prayer, Meredith was healed! God was showing her what the truth was and how to just decide in her heart to believe. It was so simple, and she was so thankful, she could spend the day playing with her kids instead of lying in her bed.

Discussion Questions

1. Have you ever shied away from praying with someone?

2. Have you ever seen God heal instantly?

3. How did the healing affect your relationship with God?

Pray for restoration of health and wholeness for one of your patients or someone you know.

Prayer Example

God of mercy and love. We stand on your promises. We believe and proclaim that by your son Jesus's stripes we are truly healed. We boldly come to you in thanksgiving that you are restoring health and wholeness to (your patient's name) and bringing glory to your name. We pray all this in your son's precious, powerful, and holy name. Amen.

CHAPTER 4

When God Doesn't Heal Right Away

What if our prayers do not get answered? Sometimes God is not saying "no," he is saying, "Not right now." As a society, we are not accustomed to waiting. Sometimes that old saying "Good things come to those who wait" is absolutely true. I am reminded of a scripture in 2 Peter 3:8, "For with the Lord one day is as a thousand years, and a thousand years is as one day." It is clear that God's timetable may not fit into our own timetable. However, the waiting can be the hardest part. Take the story of Abraham and Elizabeth, for example. They were promised a son when Abraham was 75 years old. But it did not happen that year or the next year or the next. As a matter of fact, it would be 25 more years before they would actually see that promise come to pass. That is right, I said 25 years, making Abraham 100 years old. Most of us can't even wait 25 minutes for something. Often, we lose our faith and give up on our hopes and dreams. Has this ever happened to you? My husband experienced this firsthand after he became paralyzed in his early twenties.

It was the summer of 2002; my husband and I were young newlyweds living in our first one-bedroom apartment in Virginia Beach. I had just graduated with my nursing degree and started working full time as an ED nurse in a Catholic community hospital in Norfolk, Virginia. My husband Nick was a full-time college student, an intern at NASA Langley, and a waiter on the weekends. That summer he suddenly began to suffer from excruciating lower back pain. It was as if someone was stabbing him and, oddly, it only occurred late in the night when he was trying to sleep. Teasingly, I told him it was because he was spending too much of his time sitting at that computer of his. I gave him some Motrin and a heating pad, but it only got worse keeping him awake in agony all night and then his day would start all over again with hardly any rest.

We decided to make an appointment with our doctor, and she thought maybe it was a pinched nerve. Dr. Sinclair prescribed physical therapy and anti-inflammatory medication. I thanked God my job provided us with decent medical insurance because like most 22-year-olds, we were young, broke, and in debt with student loans. After a few weeks of physical therapy, he continued to decline. His legs started to feel like lactic acid pain, which we attributed to running. But then his legs began to go out on him causing him to spontaneously collapse periodically throughout the day. The first time it happened he was walking between college classes on campus. It was as if his legs just stopped working and he just fell right there on the sidewalk. He was able to get back up but could barely feel his feet. His back pain was unbearable. He began to feel pins and needles, as if your limb had fallen to sleep. Conditions were changing rapidly and then he lost feeling in his lower legs. Even though he would never admit it, I could tell he was afraid. His parents gave him an old pair of crutches to get around and keep him from falling.

I remember getting down on my knees and praying for his pain to go away night after night. Sleepless nights turned into sleepless weeks. He didn't sleep and neither did I. The circles under our eyes were getting darker by the day. At his next physical therapy visit, his therapist didn't like the way things were looking. He decided to cancel Nick's session and instructed him to see Dr. Sinclair again. We went back to see Dr. Sinclair and this time she ordered an MRI to see what was going on inside. She went on to prescribe a handicap car decal and a wheelchair. Nick reluctantly accepted the handicap decal but was way too stubborn to accept a wheelchair. He was stubbornly not giving up and fought to earn his bruises from falling rather than do the right thing.

I will never forget that morning. The MRI was scheduled first thing at 7:00 a.m. on a Saturday. I had to drive Nick because he couldn't feel his feet. We finished the MRI and decided to go out for breakfast before heading back to the apartment. We had only been home for a few minutes before the phone rang. Nick answered it with a concerned look on his face. Then he sat down on the bed. I asked him, "Who is it?" I thought to myself, this can't be good. As the person continued to talk to him, his face, posture, and whole demeanor just sank. He handed the phone to me and said, "You talk to her, I just can't," and started weeping. I was shocked, I had never seen him cry before.

I picked up the phone and to my surprise, it was Dr. Sinclair. I spoke up, "Hello, Dr. Sinclair, this is Jen. What is going on?" She asked if I was sitting down. I sat down on our bed and prepared myself for the very worst. She continued to explain that Nick's MRI revealed a very large spinal cord tumor pressing on all of his nerves. Suddenly, everything seemed to be happening in slow motion. I could hear her young children playing in the background; she was calling from her house on her day off. I immediately had questions, "Is it benign, has it spread? I asked her to repeat the name of the tumor, so I could write it down. She went on, "It is an ependymoma. We won't know if it is benign or malignant until the biopsy."

She continued to inform us of the neurosurgeon for whom she had made a referral, Dr. Grant Skidmore. She highly recommended him and stated Nick would need neurosurgery urgently. I followed up with more questions, "Will he have to take chemo or radiation? She said, "We would know more after the biopsy and surgery. If it was benign and they could remove it all, he might not need chemo or radiation. If it were malignant then he might need chemo and/or radiation depending on the type of cancer." I was in shock; we never expected a tumor. Dr. Sinclair could tell I was in full-on nurse mode, trying to be strong and brave for my husband. She tried to let me off the hook by telling me, "It's okay, you don't have to be a nurse right now, and it is okay if you are upset." I knew she was right, but I needed to be strong for my husband. I politely thanked her and wrote down Dr. Skidmore's phone number. Then we hung up.

Just like that our whole world had fallen apart. All of our hopes and dreams were gone. All of our challenging college courses, internships, and side hustles no longer mattered. There was so much uncertainty. Would he survive this? Would he be in a wheelchair for the rest of his life? would we even be able to have children one day? We were in our early twenties and had only been married for two years. Then in one phone call, all our youthful invincibility had just melted away like a snowflake in the sun. Suddenly, we could feel the weight of our own mortality at the young ages of 21 and 23. Nick started to absorb what had just happened and flooded me with questions, "What did she say? What kind of cancer is it?"

"Some kind of tumor I've never heard of called an ependymoma," I explained. More questions followed. "Is the nerve damage permanent? What if I have to get radiation, will we even be able to have kids?" I confessed; I didn't know. We just held each other. I promised him we were going to get through this together. That afternoon, we scoured my nursing books and what was available on the internet at that time for answers. Unfortunately, this type of tumor was so rare that there was very little research or information about it.

For years, Nick didn't really share this next part of the story with our friends. He was always worried that people might think he was a little crazy. But as we grow in our faith, we are learning that God is using our stories for His glory.

The next day as the shock had worn off a little, Nick's eyes got wide and he looked at me as though he had just seen a ghost. I asked him what was the matter? He said, "Oh no, Jen, I just realized this is what that dream was about; it is actually happening!"

"What dream," I asked. Remember, it was about two years ago, when I woke you early in the morning in a cold sweat?" As I thought about it, I did remember that night. I felt a chill rush through my body as goose bumps appeared on my arms.

I remembered Nick waking me up out of a dead sleep around three in the morning a couple of years back. He was shaking me with an intense look, something I had never seen on his face before, saying, "Wake up, wake up!" The way he was shouting you would have thought the building was on fire or someone was trying to break into our apartment. I had never seen him react to a dream. We ended up talking about it for a while that night trying to figure out what it meant. At the time we didn't really know what to make of the dream. Now two years had passed, and I couldn't remember all the details. "What had happened in that dream?" I asked.

"Remember, at first, I was walking into the ocean, and I can't explain it, but I felt something bad absorbed into my body that was going to kill me. I knew I was going to die. Next, I was lying in a hospital bed with a gown on and a white sheet on me. The doctors were trying to figure out what was wrong with me. In my dream I couldn't move, I was paralyzed from the waist down! Then someone surrounded by a blinding bright light came walking across the hospital room from a distance. It was strange the way the light would change as he moved pass objects. It was weird, the light was so blinding I couldn't see his face. This reminded me of the scripture in Exodus 33:20 when God says to Moses, `You cannot see my face, for man shall not see me and live.' Then, he spoke in a sort of booming but warm, deep, and gentle voice. He said to me, `You must have absolute faith, or you will surely die.'"

As Nick spoke of the memory from that night, it came flooding back to me. It gave me even more chills. "Oh, my word, this is really happening," I said putting my hand over my mouth. But Nick was the love of my life, I was not about to lose him. "Okay, well that is it," I declared; "We are going to have absolute faith!" I really didn't know what it would feel like to have our faith tested. It was a good thing that God had already given us some faith. In Romans 12:3 it says to "think with sober judgment, each *according to the measure of faith that God has assigned.*"

We did not really have a church of our own at that time, but we did occasionally attend Nick's parents' church. We decided to meet with the elders of the church to pray for us. I did not expect to be so emotional but the moment we asked for prayers, I couldn't hold the tears back. They brought us to a private room and five elderly men in suits came in. They first read the scripture James 5:14, which states, "Is any sick among you? Let him call for the elders of the church: and let them pray over him, anointing him with oil in the name of the Lord." Then they applied a small amount of olive oil to a white handkerchief and placed it on my husband's forehead. Next, all of the elders laid hands on my husband and prayed out loud for my husband's upcoming surgery and for his healing. It was very comforting and humbling at the same time to share our needs and ask for help. My husband said, in that moment when the elders had their hands on him and were praying over him, he could feel God's presence; it was like God was right there in the middle of the prayer circle. He felt surrounded and covered with warmth. Afterwards he told me, "I could feel the hope and the light."

The next week, we had an appointment to meet the neurosurgeon that Dr. Sinclair had recommended. That week crept by slower than molasses going uphill in January, but at last we were finally going to get some answers. We met with Dr. Grant Skidmore in his office for the first time. We found him to be very wise, knowledgeable, and kind. He first sat down to talk with us and learn about the symptoms Nick was having. Then he assessed his pain and afterwards we discussed the MRI results. When he read the MRI report his thick eyebrow raised a bit, and he seemed to hold back for a moment to carefully decide on the exact words to say next. I think we both must have been holding our breath on what he was about to share. Then he confessed, "I'm going to be honest with you; you have one of the largest spinal cord tumors I've ever seen, and I have seen a lot of spinal tumors."

Well, as you might imagine, those words did not provide us a speck of comfort. Then he went on to discuss the urgency of removing it sooner than later. Dr. Skidmore stated that these tumors are usually benign, but we wouldn't know for sure until the surgery. He went on to describe how he would need to cut a little above it and a little below the tumor to remove all of it. As a nurse I knew just how risky this surgery was. The tumor originated from his lower spinal cord and went down to squeeze all of the lower nerve branches. One wrong cut and Nick could be paralyzed for life. The fear of the unknown was surreal. We needed to have faith, but the fear was real. Nobody said it would be so hard or so scary.

Each day dragged on for what felt like an eternity. To add to the chaos, a sewage leak sprung up in our apartment. Most of the living room carpet, vinyl bathroom floors, and walls would all have to be replaced. In addition, we'd have to be moving furniture regularly to cope with all of the renovation. All of this, of course, would all occur as Nick was scheduled to come home from his extensive back surgery. We were thinking of moving in with Nick's parents to help care for Nick after the surgery. I had just started my nursing job in the ER and did not have enough paid time off. Even though our lease was not up for several months, Nick and his dad went over to the property manager and asked to see if they would let us out of our lease given the circumstances. Nick and his dad returned victoriously. They let us out of the lease without any penalties. Now all we had to do was move.

We stayed busy, moving. Well, I stayed busy moving. Nick watched in severe pain as his friends and family helped us move back into Nick's parent's house. The day of the surgery finally came two weeks later. Nick's pain was intense, and I was so glad that God could move mountains with just the faith the size of a tiny mustard seed, because to be honest, that was all it felt like we had. But even during the waiting God was there. When the doctors couldn't provide much reassurance, God somehow could provide the deeper peace and the comfort we needed. At that point God was really all we had left. We had absolutely no control over any part of this whole situation.

Nick was so glad to finally be getting rid of this large tumor he teasingly had named Mini Focker in reference to the movie *Meet the Parents*. We woke up early the next morning at around 3:00 am, so we could be at the hospital by 5 a.m. to prepare for surgery. Pastor Randy from the church met us early that morning in the preoperative area to pray over him. He prayed over Nick, his body, his doctors, and nurses. Then when it was time for Nick to go into the OR, Pastor Randy left, and Nick's parents and I were directed to the plainly decorated beige waiting room. There we waited, and as we waited it felt like the clock on the wall was literally standing still. Nick's mom kept reassuring me that all was going to be well, but still you could feel the hidden anxiety in the atmosphere.

Finally, some nine hours later, around 2 p.m. the doctor arrived to update us and let us know how it went. He was smiling and very hopeful that all was well. He said he was able to remove all of the tumor and it was fully encapsulated. He would send it to the lab for testing. Soon we would be able to go and be with Nick. After 30 minutes a nurse came to bring us back to see Nick. Only I could go back to see him at first. It was hard to see him in a hospital bed; he looked so sleepy. When Nick saw me, he smiled from ear to ear and urged me to touch his feet. He wanted to know if he could feel them. "I can feel them, I can feel them!" He looked so relieved. The nurse began to ask if Nick could tell her his name and today's date; he declared he was the Queen of England and it was 1802 before cracking a smile and winking at me.

I wish I could tell you that it was the end. I wish I could tell you he was miraculously healed that day and stood and walked out of the hospital just like in John 5:8 when Jesus saith unto him, the healed paralyzed man, "Rise, take up your bed, and walk." While it did become Nick's favorite verse, the truth is Nick spent a week in the hospital and then several excruciating months at home recovering and learning to walk again. Thank goodness we had moved back in with Nick's parents, because even with insurance, we soon found out we could not afford all of the medical bills. Nick's pain continued to be intense and lasted for many years afterwards. He worked hard at learning to walk again, and we were happy with that. We had given up on Nick ever being able to run, pick me up, or wrestle with our future children one day.

Nick went on to finish his bachelor's degree and we moved to Georgia to be closer to my parents and pursue better job opportunities. Over time the pain wore on Nick's spirits and it was so hard for me to watch him in pain all the time. He was attending physical therapy and I was holding us together by a thread financially. The combination was stressful on our marriage. But we decided life was short, so we should have children sooner than later. In August of 2004, we had a beautiful little girl and named her Brooklynn. Nick got an entry-level job with a good company. Three years flew by and before we knew it, we were pregnant with a sweet little baby boy. This time we already knew what we wanted to name him, Grant. After Dr. Grant Skidmore who had removed Nick's spinal cord tumor.

Soon we found a good church and started going there regularly. Then I read a book called *The Power of a Praying Wife* by Stormy Omartian. It caused me to pray for my husband in a different way, and I wish I could tell you that the next day he changed overnight. The funny thing is, I think I changed just as much as he did. However, these changes did not occur on my timetable. It took about six months to a year, but gradually something came alive inside of Nick. He went back to school and finished his master's degree. He started to push himself in ways he hadn't before. He started waking up early Saturday mornings and running with a friend, Wayne, at a nearby high school football field. Even though it hurt to run he pushed on through the pain. He joined a gym and started working out. He rounded up some guys, like his great friend Saurabh, at work and decided to go hike Mount Washington in New Hampshire. Then they turned that one experience into an annual adventure where they constantly push themselves. The change was so gradual that it happened over the years right in front of me.

It was about 12 years to be exact, which is about half of the time Abraham would have to wait for his promised child. It was September of 2014; we had decided to take the kids on a vacation to see the giant trees in the Sequoia National Park in California. It was there while we were on vacation that it finally dawned on me. God had not only restored Nick's health, but Nick was now healthier, more spiritual, and fitter than he had ever been prior to the spinal cord tumor. Tears filled my eyes as I shared this epiphany with my husband. I was reminded of the story of Job in the Bible. Specifically, how in the story of Job all had been taken from him, but in the end, God not only restored all that was lost but gave him twice what he had before.

Nick could now pick me up and wrestle with his kids. He was not just walking but hiking mountains and running the Peachtree Road Race in Atlanta! As a matter of fact, this past summer my husband did the impossible. He and his friend Saurabh hiked 16 hours round trip to the tallest summit in the continental United States, Mount Whitney, at a breathtaking 14,508 feet high! Job 5:18 states, "For He wounds, but He binds up; He shatters, but His hands heal." I know that in the beginning that spinal cord tumor looked like it was meant for my husband's harm, but truly it made him the man God created him to be today. God took what little faith we had and grew it. In James 1:2 it says, "Count it all joy, my brothers, when you meet trials of various kinds, for you know that the testing of your faith produces steadfastness." Notice James didn't say *if* you meet trials, but "**when**" you meet trials of various kinds. Don't give up in your times of trouble. Your real faith can only come into fruition during the difficult times. Furthermore, your circumstances do not define your faith.

Discussion Questions

1. Have you ever had to wait a long time for God to answer your prayer?

2. How did you grow in the waiting season?

3. How do you stay encouraged during the waiting?

Pray for God to give you strength and endurance during the waiting seasons. Thank Him that He is growing your faith and providing peace, healing, and restoration.

Prayer Example

Heavenly Father, let your Holy Spirit shine like a bright light into _____'s body bringing forth healing, forgiveness, peace, comfort, and restoration. Wrap your loving arms around _____ and allow the peace that surpasses all understanding to wash over him/her. Help him/her to trust in your will and your timing even when it doesn't align with our own timing. Father, we know you can use all things for good and this was not a surprise to you. Thank you for growing us through our struggles and giving us the victory. In Jesus's name. Amen.

CHAPTER 5

Illness Used for Salvation

Sometimes God uses our setbacks to set us up for something better. Sometimes He even uses our illness to bring us closer to Him. This happened to my mother-in-law, Debbie. Back in January of 1997, Debbie discovered a lump in her left breast. She had had a mammogram and doctors said they just wanted to watch it. That is just what they did, and she had a mammogram every year.

Back in September 1996, I had just met the love of my life, Debbie's son Nick. We were high school sweethearts. Debbie had been working out in the early part of the year and was successfully losing weight. Then, like most of us with good intentions, she fell off the wagon and stopped working out. But oddly enough she was still losing weight. Debbie put two and two together and decided to follow up with her doctor. Nick and I had dated for about another year or so before Debbie's doctor became concerned and wanted to perform a biopsy. He called her back to schedule an appointment to go over the biopsy results with her. As she feared, it was not good. He diagnosed her with breast cancer in July of 1997 and told her, "This is going to be the roughest year of your life."

When I met Nick, he and his parents believed in God, but that was really the extent of their faith. They were your average American military working family. As she looks back now, Debbie says, "I knew of God, but I didn't really *know* Him." Nick's dad, Todd, admits, "I always believed but I would struggle with the ways of the world. I was sort of flopping around in my faith. I never really shared the good news with anyone. I kind of hid my light under a bushel so to speak." They would go to Debbie's parents church every once in a while. When I first met Debbie prior to her breast cancer, she was sort of a perfectionist. She took a lot of pride in the way that she looked. She was the kind of woman who never had a hair out of place. You would never catch her without all her makeup on, she was always dressed nice, wore high heels, and her nails always looked beautiful.

Like a lot of women, she spent a lot of time all caught up in the way she looked and, like most of us, she often would criticize her appearance.

Little did she know; this cancer was about to change everything. Debbie and Todd both immediately went home and got down on their knees and prayed to God. They pleaded with Him for more than an hour. Todd made a promise to God right then and there to read the entire Bible and be a witness to the people God placed before him. He did go on to read the entire Bible cover to cover. Even to this day, Todd has never met a stranger. He often befriends others out in public and tells them the good news of Christ and prays with them.

They scheduled Debbie to receive a radical mastectomy. They would be removing the entire left breast, the muscle layer beneath it, and any involved lymph nodes. In the recovery room the doctor shared the results of the surgery. The tumor itself was rather large, about 4 cm by 6 cm, and had spread to thirteen lymph nodes. They removed all thirteen of them, all the breast tissue, and the left chest muscle layer. They had taken so much the leftover skin was stretched paper thin just to close the incisions. She had multiple drains poking out of the incision.

Debbie just knew she was a goner. Afterall, her mom died just four short years after being diagnosed with the same kind of cancer back in 1981. "I saw what she went through, and I just didn't want to go that way." Her mom had also had a total mastectomy, but she didn't even have any cancer in any of her lymph nodes. Debbie's cancer was worse because it had already spread to thirteen lymph nodes. If her mom died without any lymph node involvement, what kind of chance would Debbie have?

But then again, maybe her mom had just given up after her dad decided it was all just too much and started courting another woman while her mom was undergoing treatment for cancer. "What hope did she have, even if she survived, her husband was going to leave her." For years Debbie assumed stress had caused her mom's cancer. Prior to the cancer she had just lost her son, Debbie's brother, to suicide after recovering from a severe motor vehicle accident. But later Debbie would discover she herself tested positive for the BRCA2 gene putting her and probably her mom at risk for breast cancer. So now what? She would have a month to recover from surgery. Then the doctor recommended chemotherapy starting that September every other week for six weeks.

They first had to grow her stem cells with Neupogen shots. Once she had extra, they harvested her stem cells, irradiated them, and then grew them in a lab. "When they harvest your stem cells, they put you on this machine, like a dialysis machine. It filters your blood to pull out your stem cells and then it puts the blood back into you." Well, while Debbie was in the middle of this procedure, the machine broke down. Half of her blood was in the machine and half was in her. She thought to herself, "This is going to kill me, my blood is going to coagulate before they can put it back. I am going to die right here on this broken machine!" Then the lady assigned to her had to get on the phone with someone long distance to fix the machine! Finally, the machine starts working again. Debbie survived her surgery and now her stem cell harvesting. They ended up collecting 5 million cells, they only needed 2 million.

Now she was ready to start her three doses of regular chemotherapy, followed up with three days of high-dose chemo. "The same kind of chemo they give to patients with leukemia." I remember that Thanksgiving, it was the first time my parents had invited Nick's parents to dinner. Debbie's immune system was so weak. We had to make sure there weren't any fresh foods, fresh flowers, or germs anywhere. We sanitized our entire house thoroughly, especially the kitchen and dining room. I was a little nervous and excited for our parents to have dinner for the first time. It turned out to be a warm, peaceful, and enjoyable meal. Our parents seemed to get along well. It was good to see Debbie smiling and eating.

After the high-dose chemotherapy for 6 hours a day for 3 days, her doctor told her she would probably get so sick she would end up hospitalized. By this point, Debbie dwindled down to nothing. She stood 5 foot 8 inches and weighed only 106 pounds. She was so sick she couldn't eat anything. The only thing she could stomach was chicken bouillon broth. After the chemotherapy, she was scheduled to receive a bone marrow transplant of her own stem cells on December 5th. While they were performing the bone scan, there were spots all over the scan. It lit up like a Christmas tree. "It scared the dickens out of me; I thought, good Lord, this cancer is just everywhere. I just knew I was going to die. I realized I could not do this in my own strength."

After her stem cells were transplanted back into her body, they had to wait and see if they would grow back. If they grew back, she would live, but if they didn't, she would die. Unfortunately, Debbie's stem cells were not growing back. She was admitted to the hospital within just five short days on December 10th. Her platelets were too low; her blood was pooling and leaking inside her.

"I had petechiae, little blood spots, all over my body; it looked like someone had beat me with a wire brush all over. They told me if I stubbed my toe, I could bleed to death. My dad and husband wanted to come see me every day, but I just didn't want anyone to see me like that. I was so sick and weak; I couldn't even make it from the bed to the bathroom."

She was so embarrassed to call for a nurse to come clean her up. After two weeks, she started getting better and she was able to go home at 6 p.m. on Christmas Eve to be with her family. It was a Christmas miracle for sure.

In the meantime, Satan was working on her telling her she was not going to make it. Debbie started planning for her death. She didn't go out and buy clothes or spend money on herself. She started throwing personal things out that she did not want her family to have to deal with after she died. She even threw away her high school yearbook. This fear had crept in and set up shop in her mind.

Then God would send her a coworker or friend, who would give her scripture such as Isaiah 53:5's "and with His stripes we are healed." And Debbie intentionally clung to those scriptures. There was a preacher she started listening to named Andrew

Womack who preached a lot on healing. "It was after I started listening to those healing messages, I started to change my way of thinking." Her faith began to grow, she started to believe that God was her rock, and He was strengthening her. It was then she stopped relying on what the tests said and started relying on what God says. She and Todd found a good church and started attending regularly.

A friend, Elaine, really helped her keep her eyes focused on the Lord. She would tell me, "It didn't matter what man says, it matters what God says." Debbie said, "I felt God put the right people in my path to help me when I needed it most." James 5:16 states, "Therefore confess your sins to one another and pray for one another, that you may be healed. The prayer of a righteous person has great power as it is working." Another friend, Linda, who's heart was failing and was in need of a heart transplant inspired her. She spoke of the scripture in Matthew 14:34–36:

> "And when they had crossed over, they came to the land at Gennesaret. And when the men of that place recognized him, they sent around to all that region and brought to him all who were sick and implored him that they

> might only touch the fringe of
> his (Jesus's) garment. As many as
> touched it were made well."

Linda would just imagine she was touching His garment or smelling it. So, Debbie decided, she needed to try this too. Linda had the elders at the church pray over her too. Her friend ended up being healed without ever receiving that heart transplant. Linda was a great inspiration to Debbie. Another friend told her to think about these things that are happening, take them, and look at them like an object, say a shirt or a blouse. In the same way you might lay a shirt or blouse out on a table, lay out or set before God all your troubles and then just give them to God like you were giving a shirt to your friend.

That January, Debbie was sentenced to receiving six grueling weeks of radiation to her left chest. She knew her heart and her lungs were also getting zapped with each treatment. She would hope and pray her heart and lungs would be okay. She used to imagine Jesus sitting next to her when she was going through the treatment.

> "I would lay down and wait for the
> buzzer to go off for the radiation;
> that buzzer, it was just a terrible,
> terrible sound. Then I looked up

and saw that the ceiling tile formed a cross. So, I just kept my mind focused on the cross. I knew that Jesus was with me. That helped get me through that."

Finally, about two months later she finished her radiation treatment. In a couple of weeks, it would be time to go back for a checkup to see the results of the last scan. Maybe after all this, she would be cured! The next week she went to see her doctor only to find out it had spread to her ribs instead. That's right, despite the surgery, the chemo, the bone marrow transplant, the radiation, and the prayers, the cancer had survived and spread to her ribs. The bad news was there was nothing else the doctors could do right now. Her body was far too weak; if they gave her chemo or radiation now, it would surely kill her. All she could do now is wait; it would be at least three more months before they could try more chemo or radiation.

I remember looking out the back-door thinking, "How do you get ready to die? You can't pack a suitcase, nobody can come with you, and it's a one-way trip. You're going by yourself. That was the moment, I decided I am not going." After a couple of months, Debbie and Todd continued praying, going to church, and reading the Bible.

Debbie had read James 5:14 that states: "Is anyone among you sick? Let him call for the elders of the church and let them pray over him with oil in the name of the Lord." So, the Sunday before her next doctor's appointment, she and Todd asked their pastor, Randy, for the elders at their church to pray over her. After church service the elders took Debbie to a private room in the back and laid hands on her. They anointed her head with olive oil. Each one of them said a special prayer over Debbie.

> "I really felt the Lords' presence in that room in that moment, more than any other time ever in my life. I felt really happy, like He was with me, all my worries, despair, and fears suddenly left me. But I still had this feeling, I just didn't feel like I was good enough to be in His presence."

A few days after the elders prayed over Debbie, she was scheduled to get another scan to see what the damage was to her ribs. Depending on the results of the scan, she would have to get more surgery, chemotherapy, and/or radiation. After the scan they had scheduled an appointment to go over the results. To everyone's surprise the scan came back clean. There was no more cancer! The doctors were confused. The previous scan clearly showed areas of cancer in her ribs and the new scan showed absolutely none. She was healed! Without more radiation, without more chemo, without more surgery, she was cured by Jesus's stripes.

In the midst of sickness, trials, and tribulation, it might appear as though nothing good can come from this pain. But God can use our pain, sickness, trial, or tribulations to deepen and grow our knowledge of Him. It was the cancer that caused Debbie, Todd, and her son Nick to seek and find Christ. Sometimes, "God is not trying to pay you back; He is trying to bring you back," as Pastor Bart Stone said. Maybe this is what Peter meant in 1Peter 1:6–7:

> "In this you rejoice, though now for a little while, if necessary, you have been grieved by various trials, so that the tested genuineness of your faith—more precious than gold that perishes though it is tested by fire—may be found to result in praise and glory and honor at the revelation of Jesus Christ."

Today, over two decades later, Debbie is still with us enjoying each day with her grandkids she never thought she would see. Today her faith and trust are stronger still in the Lord. She isn't easily shaken over medical tests or trials of this world. Looking back Debbie realizes God's perfect timing in everything. God waited until there was no other treatment that could be done by man, to prove without a doubt to Debbie and her doctors that it was God alone that healed her. It ultimately grew Debbie's faith and demonstrated to her His power and glory. "It really opened my eyes." She knew it was not her own strength or even her doctors that healed her. She is reminded of scripture that states, "What is it if a man gains all the riches of the world but loses his soul?" The cancer that was meant to be the death of her, turned out to be her saving grace.

Discussion Questions

1. How is God trying to bring you closer to Him?

2. Have you ever seen God use a difficult situation to bring good in your own life?

Pray for God to help you trust more. Thank Him that He is working all things for His glory even the bad things.

Prayer Example
Practice writing your own prayer on the lines below.

_____

_____

_____

_____

_____

_____

_____

_____

_____

CHAPTER 6

How to Pray

A few years ago, we were at home after a busy work and school day, when we received a surprising text. The text was inviting anyone who wanted to come and pray for a couple tonight at their home. We instantly recognized this couple and learned our friend Kayleen had just been given a very poor prognosis for what appeared to be advanced stage pancreatic cancer. Our friends were in their thirties with three young children. Kayleen and her husband, Tommy, were very active with our church serving on the kids check-in team, hosting life groups, and even singing with the band. Both our eldest children were in the same grade. Nick and I immediately decided we should go and pray with them. It was the first time I had ever seen or participated in a healing prayer group.

We were running a few minutes late, trying to get our own kids fed and homework done. Then of course we got lost trying to find their house. When we finally got there, I was happy to see that about 15 other cars were already parked outside their home. My husband and I were briefed on the latest developments of Kayleen's health. Basically, the doctors told Kayleen this very large pancreatic mass did not look good. They weren't sugarcoating it at all. It appeared to be the worst kind of pancreatic cancer and would need to be removed as soon as possible. The mortality rate for this particular cancer was very high. The surgery was urgently scheduled for tomorrow morning. Kayleen was saying things like, "I am not afraid to die, but I just don't want to leave my children and husband alone." We greeted everyone and after about 10 minutes we decided everyone who was coming had arrived. So, we gathered into the living room filling up all the couches, chairs, floor space, and standing room. Two of our pastors at church came with their wives and children.

Kayleen sat in the middle of the living room in a chair and everyone that was near her placed their hand on her and one of our pastors led us in prayer. Then when he was done, others around the room one-by-one spontaneously spoke up and prayed out loud for Kayleen. I remember being in wonder of how everyone else knew exactly what to say, and how to say it. They knew what to pray for, and they covered every aspect and every detail. Each person spontaneously prayed for a different aspect of Kayleen's healing. We prayed for her, her husband, her children, the doctors, for the surgery itself, and for the nurses. We even prayed for her to get a good night's sleep that night. We prayed for the ease of the pain, for peace, and for comfort. With our eyes closed and forming a circle around Kayleen, I could tangibly feel the faith and the warmth of the Holy Spirit in the room. I remember one of our pastors praying and declaring that he was boldly asking for God to remove the cancer and heal her altogether.

I had never experienced such bold, faith-filled prayers and I was in complete wonderment! I prayed with the group, but not out loud. I still wasn't comfortable praying out loud. When we arrived, the stress of the day had worn on me. But after we prayed, suddenly I was no longer tired, but full of hope and energy. We must have prayed for at least 30 minutes straight. Just when I thought we had prayed for everything, our other pastor closed us out in prayer, and I remember just being in awe of how he prayed and how thoughtful and healing his words of prayer were. I thought to myself, "Wow, I want to be able to pray like that!" But I didn't know where to start. When I think back on it, no one had ever taught me how to pray for healing or even to just pray out loud. I was comfortable praying quietly in my head when I didn't have to worry what others might think. The first step of my prayer journey was simply making myself vulnerable and pursuing how to pray out loud in front of others.

I decided to start small. I figured a few baby steps in the right direction were better than nothing at all. After all, what father is not proud of his child making progress? I decided to practice and bring my children on this prayer journey with me. We started taking turns praying out loud at the dinner table each night. I confessed my anxieties about praying out loud to a few of my close Christian friends, who graciously let me practice with them. It is good to find a mentor who can also show you the way on your prayer journey. Honestly, at first, I was not very good at praying out loud: it felt awkward. It reminded me of standing up and giving a presentation before my middle school classmates. My hands would get sweaty and my heart would start racing. But I made up my mind I was going to try anyway. It's true, that old saying, "Practice makes perfect." The more I prayed out loud the easier it became. I made a point to pray out loud daily. Soon I was able to pray with work colleagues and in small group settings even where I did not know everyone.

About a year later, I was starting to overcome the speaking out loud part, but I still wanted to know what to say and how to say it. Then I started to read books about prayer and scripture surrounding prayer. While reading Alex and Stephen Kendrick's book, The Battle Plan for Prayers, I discovered something so brilliantly simple, I wondered why I had never thought of it before. The book suggested asking God to help you learn to pray. What? You mean all this time I could have just asked my heavenly Father to help me learn to pray stronger and more effective prayers? I knew I could ask God for anything, but for some reason, it never occurred to me. I thought I had to learn to pray all in my own strength. In James 1:5, James is advising us what to do when trials and troubles come our way. He goes on to say, "If any of you lacks wisdom, let him ask God, who gives generously to all without reproach, and it will be given him." I am here to tell you, it really is just that simple, just ask your heavenly Father to help you pray.

I started practicing prayer in other ways. We all learn in various ways; I thought it might be helpful to try many prayer methods. I tried writing down my prayer targets on a chalkboard and on paper. There is also an app for that, where you can list the prayers you want to pray and set an alarm to remind you to pray at a certain time of day. I made a prayer priority list. For me my prayer priority list went something like this: God, spouse, children, friends and family, jobs, school, and ways to use my gifts for His glory. I then incorporated the A.C.T.S. of prayer. These include: Adoration, Confession, Thanksgiving, and Supplication. Philippians 4:6 states, "Do not be anxious about anything, but in everything by prayer and supplication with thanksgiving let your requests be known to God."

I also tried praying in various places and in different postures. For example, sometimes, I will go to the hospital chapel to pray quietly sitting with my head bowed. Other times I will pray out loud with my eyes open while driving to work or walking my dog. Sometimes I will pray on my knees beside my bed. Sometimes I will sit with my head bowed and pray on my front porch with a cup of tea and, sometimes, I will stand. Sometimes I will pray with my hands together or touching someone's shoulder, and other times with my hands lifted up in the air.

I will say, if you are praying out loud with a patient, friend, or family member, always ask if they would like you to pray with them first. Dr. Saliman, author of "The Prayer Prescription" article, recommends inquiring about their spiritual support or if prayer plays a role in their life first (Saliman 2010). Then once you have discussed these things, it is much easier and natural to broach the question of prayer. Just as you would respect a patient's physical boundaries, you would respect one's spiritual boundaries (Saliman 2010).

That being said, we live in a scientific and politically correct world. Although most doctors and nurses will admit to having seen miracles of healing, few ever make any attempt to understand them. The goal is for His love to shine through us like an open door on a dark night during our patient's most difficult life situations. As a friend, caregiver, or a healthcare professional there are some words that are helpful to healing. Then there are other words, though well-meaning, that may be perceived as hurtful. Below is a table of some helpful Prayer do's and don'ts I have gathered along the way.

Do Say or **Do** This	**Don't** Say nor Do This
Do say, "I am here for you." Then actually listen with deep understanding and love.	Don't say, "I feel it is my duty to see or talk with you."
Do say, "This must be hard for you. I am so sorry for your loss" following the death of a loved one.	Don't say, "God needed another angel" following the death a loved one.

Do say, "Don't give up until you have tried everything. Would you like me to pray with you?"	Don't say, "This might sound crazy, but...."
Do show the love of Jesus to others and bare one another's burdens. Love is the key that opens the doors of hearts and minds.	Don't say, "You can't think that way. Or you just need to have more faith." Don't' ignore, belittle, or criticize the patient.
Do be inviting and re-spectful. Ask if prayer is part of their spiri-tual walk. Always ask first if they would like you to pray with them.	Don't pray out loud for a patient who declines prayer or has a headache with phonophobia.
Do take care of your-self mentally, physi-cally, and spiritually. Eat healthy, sleep eight hours, exercise regularly, drink 8 cups of water daily, read God's word and pray.	Don't attempt to pray for others while you're hurting or in pain.

Do pray for an increase in your own faith and understanding of prayer. Give to God anything you can't handle or understand.	Don't take on more burdens greater than what your own spiritual strength and development can bear.
Do forgive others and yourself. Take time to confront and confess your own sins to yourself, to God, and maybe to a trusted friend or spiritual advisor.	Don't harbor anger, unforgiveness, or resentment.
Do trust in God, no matter what. Trust grows with relationships. Take time to develop this relationship with God; read God's word, pray, and talk to Him.	Don't worry. God is bigger than this problem and bigger than any illness or bad medical report.
Do pray from the heart with earnest concern for the person in need.	Don't pray in vain repetitions or to show off in front of others (Matthew 6:7).

Do say, "Thank you" that you are _____." Praying with thanksgiving and supplication releases your faith in God.	Don't complain often in your prayers, it demonstrates a lack in faith and doubt of His love for us.

In Luke 11:1 KJV, the disciples approached Jesus and asked the same question, how should they pray. You may have heard of the Lord's Prayer before, but have you ever analyzed what Jesus is teaching us about prayer? As I mentioned earlier, like the disciples asked, you too can ask God how to pray. I like the old King James Version of the Lord's Prayer (Luke 11:2–4 KJV):

And Jesus said to them:

> "When you pray, say: 'Our Father which art in heaven, Hallowed be thy name. Thy kingdom come. Thy will be done, as in heaven, so in earth. Give us day by day our daily bread. And forgive us our sins; for we also forgive every one that is indebted to us. And lead us not into temptation; but deliver us from evil.'"

There are several key factors Jesus is recommending we use when we pray.

When it comes to effective healing prayers they ultimately begin with God and not you. So just relax and take the pressure and focus off yourself and what you are doing. Place all your thoughts with God. Fix your eyes on Him. Forget about everything else in this world for just a moment and connect with our heavenly Father. The word "Father" is used revealing the close and personal relationship we have with God. Prayer accesses the very presence of God. You are reaching beyond the physical into the spiritual realm. There is a sweet release when we let go and let God. Just breathe and know that we serve the God who holds all authority in Heaven and Earth.

When Jesus says, "Hallowed be thy name," he is referring to the fact that we serve an all-powerful and mighty God. "Hallowed" means revered, respected, celebrated, honored, blessed, and sacred above all names. In Proverbs 18:10 it states, "The name of the Lord is a strong tower." He is Jehovah Jireh, "The Lord Our Provider." He is the "Alpha and the Omega," the beginning and the end. He is "the Great Physician." He is the great "I Am." He is our Redeemer. He is the Creator of this great universe and He made our flesh bodies and the souls within them. He certainly doesn't need us, but through prayer we are communicating with

Him and creating an opportunity for others to see His glory firsthand. It starts by first immersing ourselves in God and then our patients or loved ones.

Next, access Gods' healing power by inviting God's Holy Spirit into the equation. Say something like, "Lord, let your Holy Spirit be present in this place." You may also acknowledge that God's Holy Spirit is life-giving and ever present within us. In 1st Corinthians 6:19 it states, "Or do you not know that your body is a temple of the Holy Spirit within you, whom you have from God? You are not your own, for you were bought with a price." You may find it helpful to visualize His healing spirit shining through you and into your patient. For life is connected through the Holy Spirit. Even before the days of Noah, Adam lived 930 years. Then in Genesis 6:3 God says, "*My Spirit shall not abide in man forever, for he is flesh: his days shall be 120 years.*" Did you catch that? It is God's spirit that has the power to allow a man to live 900+ years. As you invite his Holy Spirit in, you may feel a certain peace, lightness, radiating warmth, or calmness that comes over you.

Praying with the right heart can be more powerful than praying with the right words. So, make sure your heart is in the right place. Jesus says, "Thy Kingdom come." Jesus is teaching us to seek to further His kingdom, not our own kingdoms.

If what you are asking brings glory to God's kingdom, your prayers are more likely be answered. Pastor Bart Stone puts it like this, "As humans we tend to build our little safe kingdoms out of comforts and conveniences. However, God tends to build his kingdom out of a calling with surrender, and purpose." In Matthew 6:31, Jesus is telling us not to worry about what to wear or eat or drink because our Father knows our needs. He goes on to say, "But seek first the kingdom of God and his righteousness, and all these things will be added to you."

In the Lord's Prayer, Jesus also says, "Thy will be done." We need to align with His will not necessarily our own will. 1 John 5:14–15 states:

> "And this is the confidence that we have toward Him, that if we ask anything according to His will He hears us. And if we know that He hears us in whatever we ask, we know that we have the requests that we have asked of Him."

You may be asking well, what is His will? It is really quite simple. His will is the will of a loving Father who finds great joy in his children. In John 10:10, Jesus states, "The thief comes to steal and kill and destroy. I came that they may **have life**

and have it abundantly." In Psalms 35:27, David says, "Let those who delight in my righteousness shout for joy and be glad and say for evermore, 'Great is the Lord, **who delights in the welfare of his servant.'**" The Father's will is to see His children grow in faith and strength and develop us to be all that He created us to be. Matthew 7:11 puts it this way: "Your Father in heaven give good gifts to those who ask Him." So, if you still struggle with aligning with His will, you can just ask Him. That is right, you can just ask Him. That also took me many years before I stumbled across the wonderful little fact that I could just ask God what He wanted me to pray. Again, for some reason, I thought I had to figure that out on my own as well. You can simply say, "Lord guide my words," "reveal your will to us," or "show me what to pray."

Next in the Lord's Prayer, Jesus states, "Give us day by day our daily bread." This bread we ask for daily is a provision to feed both our physical and spiritual bodies. In the physical, bread is a universal carbohydrate which the body easily converts into a source of energy. If you have ever made homemade bread without preservatives, you know that fresh bread is only good for about a day before it becomes stale. Even in the Old Testament, when God provided manna (bread) from heaven it was only good for one day. Both our physical and our spiritual bodies need this fresh source of daily energy. God's provisions are limitless and "His mercies are made anew each morning." He knows our daily needs and it is His will as a loving father to provide for us. We just need to ask. Pastor Seth Hoover pointed out, "notice Jesus did not say give me my daily bread. He said give us our daily bread. We are blessed to be a blessing to others. Our prayers should include others in need of His provisions."

Spiritually, according to John 6:51, Jesus states, "I am the living bread that came down from heaven. If anyone eats of this bread, he will live forever. And the bread that I will give for the life of the world is my flesh." When we eat the bread and drink the juice in communion as in the Last Supper, we are symbolically partaking of Jesus. In Matthew 4:4, Jesus is being tempted in the desert and is asked, "If you are the Son of God, command these stones to become loaves of bread. But he answered, 'It is written, man shall not live by bread alone, but by every word that comes from the mouth of God.'" Spiritually, we are to partake of God's word daily. Reading God's word daily will also grow your faith.

Then activate your prayers with faith. Pastor Bart Stone put it this way, "Faith not length, gives your prayer strength." Luke 17:19 says and he said to him, "Rise and go your way; your faith had made you well." It was *his faith* that made him well. You may be asking well, what exactly is faith and how do I activate it. In Hebrews 11:1 it says, "Now faith is the assurance or substance of things hoped for, the conviction (evidence) of things not seen." What then is the difference between hope and faith? The word "assurance" in the Greek means confidence or confident expectation (Zodhiates and Baker 1991). Faith requires a little action in the confidently expecting, knowing, and believing department. "But without faith it is impossible to please Him: for He that cometh to God must believe that He is, and that He is a rewarder of them that diligently seek Him," - Hebrews 11:6. Faith itself is kind of like the wind, invisible, but the response of faith is quite visible. Faith is letting go of the comfortable and embracing God's calling. Reading God's word will also help grow faith. Romans 10:17 states, "So faith comes from hearing, and hearing through the word of Christ." Now to activate your faith, it is really quite simple. Instead of saying please or pleading to restore health and provide healing, change your "please" to a "thank you."

That is right, it is really that simple! As a matter of fact, according to Jonathan Osteen, if there was a secret password to enter to receive God's Holy Spirit and blessings of healing, it would simply be "thank you." Philippians 4:6 states, "Do not be anxious about anything, but in everything by prayer and supplication with **thanksgiving** let your requests be made known to God. Say something like, "Thank you that your light is shining through me and restoring health and wholeness into Mr. Smith." I also find it helpful for you and the patient, friend, or family member to visualize the healing, whatever it may, may it be tissues mending, bones ossifying, swelling residing, pain easing, airways opening, cancer cells destroyed, infection cleansed, or blood flow restored.

Jesus also teaches us to ask for forgiveness of our sins. Both unforgiveness and sin can block our connection with God. To experience the fullness of God, we need to repent and forgive others as we have been forgiven. Jesus then closes his prayer by asking to "lead us not into temptation, but deliver us from evil." Temptations and sin can distract us from the best God has for us. Just turn on the news or social media to catch a glimpse of the evil and dark forces in this world. They are all around us. The enemy is real and taking ground daily. We need to pray offensively to protect us from our weaknesses. God has the power and authority to deliver us from evil, we just simply need to ask.

Finally, seal your prayer with "In Jesus's holy, precious, and powerful name, we pray all these things. Amen." Which, by the way, is not just something to say at the end of a prayer. Jesus is our kinsman redeemer. No one can come to the Father except through Jesus. He pleads to the Father on our behalf. When we say Amen, it means IT IS DONE, THAT IS THAT, or SO BE IT! With that in mind, when I say amen, I like to envision a shock wave going out all around me just like after a huge explosion. Then, just be still and know that He is God.

To Recap

1. Ask God to help you pray.
2. Practice praying out loud alone or with close friends and family you trust.
3. Ask permission to pray with someone first.
4. Relax and focus on God. "Fix your eyes on Him."
5. Invite His Holy Spirit in.
6. Activate your prayers with faith, thanksgiving, and visualize the healing.
7. Ask for provision, forgiveness, and deliverance from temptation.
8. Read His word.
9. Align yourself with His will.
10. Be still and know that He is God.

The next day we received another surprising text. It said that Kayleen's surgery was a success and it turned out not to be cancer at all! She had gone from, "You probably won't survive" to "Surprise it's not cancer and you will be healed up from surgery in a couple of weeks!" Her doctors were shocked! Wow, God was so good! I was learning so much more about prayer and how it allows for God to show up and show out in our lives!

Group Exercise

Practice saying the Lord's Prayer before meals 3 times daily for a week to help you memorize it. As you pray, consider each line and what Jesus is teaching us.

Discussion Questions

1. In what areas do you struggle with when it comes to praying?

2. What is the one thing that you learned or that stood out the most in this chapter?

Prayer Example

Heavenly Father of clarity and wisdom, thank you for being the guiding light on this journey in prayer. I am grateful for all the ways you are teaching me to draw near to you and communicate with you on a deeper level. Father, I welcome your Holy Spirit to guide me and lead me to pray more effectively, so that others may see your glory. Help me to be a light in time of darkness for others. Sustain my spiritual growth and remove any stumbling blocks in my path. Give me the strength to endure and mirror your love, grace, and mercy to all those you place before me. In your son's holy and precious name I pray all this. Amen.

CHAPTER 7

Trusting

Y ou may still be asking yourself, but what if the outcomes look too bleak and you are certain your patient or loved one will not have a good outcome? In nursing school, we are taught never to give false hope to patients. In the hospital we are taught to under promise, so we can over deliver great customer service. What if you yourself don't believe the outcome can get better? I faced this recently. We had another cardiac arrest patient arrive one Wednesday morning. He had received CPR in the field for nearly an hour before reaching the hospital. He was only in his mid-50s and my colleagues made comments like, "We have a dead body coming in." We all knew the odds were stacked against anyone that has been down for that long. For every minute that passes without CPR the chances of death increase by 7%–10%. Therefore, according to the American Heart Association, after 10 minutes, there is about a 70%–100% chance of death. The doctor explained what was happening to the wife and I tried to console her.

I felt the urge to ask her if she wanted me to pray with her. But then I chickened out. I was afraid if I prayed for healing and it did not work, it might damage her faith. Instead, I asked her if she wanted the chaplain to come and pray with her. She said yes, but the chaplain did not arrive in time. Her husband died. Afterwards, I felt a horrible remorse for not asking her if she wanted me to pray with her. In the beginning, I was asking myself what if I pray and it doesn't work. Afterwards, I was asking myself, what if I had prayed and it *did* work? Now, I will never know. They say our mistakes are our biggest teachers. So, I decided to learn from this. How can you pray with a total stranger for something as heavy as life and death when you don't actually believe it will happen? I didn't know it at the time, but this failure was strengthening me and helping me to do better next time.

First, I analyzed what feelings got in the way or blocked my connection with God. It is everything that Satan likes to use against us: fear, doubt, anxiety, worry, stress, anger, sadness, or bitterness. From a strictly medical standpoint, it is also every emotion that is harmful to your physical, mental, and spiritual well-being. We have known for years that continued or routine stressors such as those mentioned earlier, lead to serious medical conditions such as hypertension, heart disease, diabetes, depression, and anxiety (National Institute of Mental Health, 2019). The real battle is taking place right now within ourselves. God is not just working for us but also through us -Pastor Luke McGee. So, how do we clear a pathway to allow God's Holy Spirit to flow freely through us?

In theory it's actually quite simple. We do the exact opposite: fear not, trust, have faith, believe, take courage, and count it all joy. These instructions were so important that God repeated them throughout scripture over and over again so we might catch on. As a parent, I understand the necessity of repetition. Some days I feel like a broken record with my kids, "Brush your hair, pick up your backpack, stop arguing with your sister..." It seems like they will never catch on, until one day they do. God is way more patient than us. The phrase "fear not" appears in the KJV Bible 331 times. The phrase "be not afraid" appears 205 times in the KJV Bible. God tells us to "trust" Him 134 times. He tells us to "believe" 143 times. These instructions were not for His benefit, but for ours.

So, why is this easier said than done? Most Christians believe God is capable of healing and performing great miracles. God did it in the past; we read about them in the Bible. Yet we **doubt, fear, or worry** He is not **willing** to help us today. John 4:18 states, "There is no fear in love, but perfect love casts out fear." To cast out this fear and doubt perhaps we must remind ourselves how much He loves us. John 3:16 states, "For God so loved the world, that he **gave** his only Son." Just let that sink in for a moment. We didn't even deserve it, but He willingly sacrificed His only Son, who was perfect and without sin. As a parent, I love my children, who are far from perfect, but I love them so much, that sacrificing them would be my worst nightmare. I would rather sacrifice myself than my own children. Yet God paid the ultimate price because He loves us.

In Mark 10:14-15, people were bringing children to Jesus for him to touch, but his disciples tried to turn the children away, thinking they were being a nuisance to Jesus. However, Jesus stopped them and said, "Let the children come to me; do not hinder them, for to such belongs the kingdom of God. Truly, I say to you, whoever does not receive the kingdom of God like a child shall not enter it." What is Jesus telling us about trust and having a child-like faith?

When my children were young, they would simply trust and believe me, because I am their mother. I could tell them the sky was blue and they would repeat, "Blue." They didn't ask for evidence, understand sarcasm, or ever consider that I could be lying at that age. In our medical growth and development classes, we are taught that young children are concrete thinkers. They don't have the logical ability that adults have to think abstractly or overanalyze things. They don't need to see the data, pie charts, or Excel spreadsheets to believe a fact. When you tell them they simply believe. Sometimes the way God operates doesn't always make logical sense to us because His ways are not our ways. This childlike faith can be hard especially for those who are very intellectual and love analyzing data. It is helpful when we pray to revert back to our childlike faith and trust. But, if this is difficult for you, simply ask God to help you in this area. If this principle goes against your very nature, remember you don't have to do everything in your own strength, rely on His strength. "Ask, and it will be given to you, seek, and you will find; knock, and it will be opened to you," - Matthew 7:7.

I decided I would not let this lost opportunity be in vain. I started practicing. First, I wrote down what I might want to pray. My prayer would have gone something like this:

Heavenly Father, we come to you in complete surrender. We ask that your Holy Spirit be present in this place, inside of every person here, and guide our words. We thank you, Father, that you are providing every healthcare worker in this room with wisdom, strength, and compassion. We thank you that your healing touch is providing peace and comfort to the _____ family. Mend their hearts, Father. We trust in your will for us to have life and have it abundantly in this world and the next. We know that the number of our days on this earth, Father, you will fulfill. At this time, we boldly ask for healing and wholeness to be restored in Mr./Mrs. _____. Strengthen and restore balance in his/her body. Whether in heaven or on earth, we surrender Mr./Mrs. _____'s life unto you at this time. Thank you, Father, that you are our healer and give you all the glory. We pray all these things in Jesus's holy and precious name. Amen.

So, if you ever find yourself in a situation where you wanted to pray but didn't, analyze what were your barriers. Pray for God to help you overcome those barriers. Then practice writing down what you would have liked to pray. God is always teaching and growing us up. He can even use our mistakes for good.

I know you may be thinking, "Okay, so what if I do pray the perfect prayer and God still doesn't show up and show out, then what?", because it is not a matter of "if" but "when" trouble will occur in our lives. What if God never answers your prayer the way you wanted Him to? I think this is where trust and obedience come into play. It is easy to trust in God when everything is going good and according to plan. What is hard, what is really challenging, is to trust, worship, and be obedient to Him in times of trouble. But wow, what an impactful witness you could be to others, when you do trust, worship, and remain obedient during the hard times! True growth happens when we are pushed outside our comfort zone both physically and spiritually.

Three young men named Shadrach, Meshach, and Abednego chose to trust God in their time of trouble. In Daniel 3:14, King Nebuchadnezzar had given them an ultimatum. The three young men either had to bow down to worship the king's golden image or be cast down into a burning fiery furnace. I think the way these brave young men responded was key. In Daniel 3:17, "If this be so our God whom we serve **is able** to deliver us from the burning fiery furnace, and he will deliver us out of your hand, O king. **But if not,** be it known to you, O king, that we will not serve your gods or worship the golden image that you have set up." They knew God was able and could deliver them, but their hearts were so trusting in God, **that even if God did not decide to deliver them**, they would accept their imminent death and remain obedient to God. God did end up delivering them and in so doing made King Nebuchadnezzar realize that the God of Shadrach, Meshach, and Abednego was more powerful than any of the king's idols and statues.

The death and resurrection of Jesus is also a powerful example of how we are to trust in God even if God doesn't deliver us from our troubles, sickness, or times of difficulty. Why did God let Jesus endure all that pain, betrayal, and affliction? Why did Jesus have to die? God could have easily delivered Jesus from the hands of the Jews. Or Jesus could have decided not to trust and be obedient. But then, where would we be now? We wouldn't have the salvation that came from Jesus's death and resurrection. Sometimes our perspective is too small. He is God, He can see the bigger picture.

I heard about how a Christian lady with cancer was giving her testimony. Despite the cancer she continued to worship God in the midst of her cancer treatment. Little did she know, she would end up converting her atheist oncologist. At the end of the testimony, everyone was expecting her to say that she beat the cancer and was healed. But instead, she didn't. Even though she was not physically healed, she smiled and said, "Saving that one doctor's soul was worth it."

So, what if your prayers were not answered the way you wanted them to be? Will you have an **"even if He doesn't attitude"**? Will you trust that His plan for you is best? Will you still worship and thank Him when everything is not going well? Not everyone in the Bible was delivered from their afflictions. In Hebrews 11:35–40, it states:

> "Some were tortured, refusing to accept release, so that they might rise again to a better life. Others suffered mocking and flogging, even chains and imprisonment. They were stoned, they were sawn in two, they were killed with the sword. They went about in skins of sheep and goats, destitute, afflicted, mistreated—of whom the world was not worthy—wandering

about in the deserts and mountains, and in dens and caves of the earth. And all these though commended through their faith did not receive what was promised, since **God had provided something better for us**, that apart from us they should not be made perfect."

God is the same yesterday, today, and tomorrow; even if our circumstances change, He is still the same. Maybe the healing isn't coming. The question is, "Will you have an 'even if He doesn't' kind of trust to know that He has something better in store and can use **all** things for good?"

Discussion Questions

1. Has a situation ever looked too bleak that you thought there was not a chance for you to recover or be restored?

2. Have you ever worried that if you pray it won't work?

3. Have you ever decided not to pray with someone and later wished you had? If so, what were some of your barriers?

Pray that God would give you the courage to pray whenever you feel intimidated. Thank Him that He is strengthening your trust and is using all things for good, even the things that don't make sense.

Prayer Example

Use the lines below to practice writing your own prayer or a prayer you wished you had said previously but didn't.

_____

_____

_____

CHAPTER 8

Ears to Hear

All my life I always thought of prayer as a one-sided conversation, where I did all the talking and God did all the listening. I mean, that is how it is in church and in all the movies, right? As I began to learn more and more about prayer on this journey, I also learned that prayer can actually be a two-sided conversation. Yes, that is right; you can have a conversation with your heavenly Father through prayer.

At first, it sounded a little strange to me. In the medical field, we are taught that hearing voices is usually not a good sign. But if you think about it, it does make sense. In the Bible, Jesus talks about having ears to hear Him. In Isaiah 50:4, it states, "Morning by morning he awakens; he awakens my ear to hear as those who are taught. John 10:3 says, "The sheep hear his voice, and he calls his own sheep by name and leads them out." In Psalm 95:7–8, it states, "Today if you hear His voice, do not harden your hearts." Hearing from God is meant to be a normal part of our relationship with Him. Perhaps listening has become a lost art of prayer and we have been missing out on a deeper more intimate relationship with our heavenly Father.

I thought I would start small. I read in John Eldredge's book, *Moving Mountains*, the key to hearing God was to start small; ask something that you do not feel strongly about either way. In this way your own will would not interfere with hearing God's will. I started with a yes or no question on a matter that I did not care which way God answered. Fully surrendering to His will is required to hear from God. It took me a while to think of something. Then I thought of it, "Should I reach out to a certain friend?" For me it was not an actual voice I heard, but more of a gut feeling. The Bible often describes the voice of God as a still small voice or a gentle whisper, but for me I have never actually heard anything. I asked my pastor, Bart Stone, if he had heard of this and how can you tell that what you are hearing is from God? He suggested I test it against the Bible. He said, "Usually anything from God will align with His holy word." This made sense to me.

Next, I decided to try something a little bigger. I wanted to see what God wanted me to pray for. To hear this gentle whisper or receive this gut feeling you have to first quiet yourself and be patient. I gave myself some time, closed my bedroom door, and made myself comfortable. There I was all alone just focusing on Jesus. It took about 10–15 minutes to get my response. Which at the time felt like a long time, but really in the grand scheme of things, it is not that long to hear from the creator of the universe. All the while I just kept focusing on Jesus and asking God what He wanted me to pray for.

All of a sudden, a cute little girl about three years old appeared in my mind. I can still see her face. She had light brown skin, blonde frizzy hair, caramel eyes, and long eyelashes. I had never seen this little girl before. Then that gut feeling came again. This time it prompted me to pray for her safe travels. Wow, I didn't even know who she was or where she was going. But I decided to be obedient; I prayed for her safe travels, for protection, for comfort, for peace, and for God to be with her wherever she went. I hope I get to meet her one day, but even if I don't, I was glad to help in some small way. Sometimes, I still think of her and pray for her wherever she is.

I told my husband about this and he was kind of shocked and thought it was really interesting.

Unbeknownst to me, he decided he too was going to ask God what He wanted him to pray for. His listening prayer ended up even more fascinating than mine. The next morning, Nick was scrolling through the news on his phone when he stopped and said, "Oh my gosh! Jen this is the guy!" He showed me a picture of a middle-aged innocent black man who was pardoned from prison that very morning. I looked at him a little puzzled, "What do you mean?"

He went on to explain"

> "So, after you told me about your listening prayer, I decided to try it out myself. A few days ago, I had been praying for God to show me what to pray for. Then on the second day I prayed again for God to show me what to pray. That is when God showed me this man. At the time I had never seen him before. During my prayer I could see his face. He was weeping in a dark place by himself crying out to God and praying for innocence. I could tell he was scared. I prayed for God's spirit to be with him, I prayed he would be declared innocent, to give him strength, and

for peace and comfort to surround
him. Then to see this man was now
pardoned, wow!"

Perhaps, Nick's prayers helped that man get
through one of his darkest uncertain nights of his
life. We both just stood there in awe of God! No
one ever told us we could ask God what to pray
for and we could help complete strangers anywhere in need. What a beautiful gift we never
knew existed.

Today, I was thanking God for the restful season we were currently in and how much I really appreciated having more time off to spend
with my family. The past three years had been
more like a marathon; at times I barely had time
to spend with friends, write, or even get some
much-needed rest. But recently, I dropped down
to part-time work and my oldest daughter was
now driving herself to school and practices. With
all this free time, distractions could easily find a
way of creeping in and setting up shop. The older
I get the more I realize how fast time passes and
I often catch myself wondering where it went. I
decided to ask God what He wanted me to do with
my newfound free time. I honestly just wanted to
do whatever was pleasing to Him. Lo and behold,
that gut feeling told me to finish this book. So, I
turned off the TV and put my paint brushes up

and got back to writing. Who knows, maybe my prayer journey will help someone in need and together we can bring forth God's light of hope and healing to others all over the world?

Discussion Questions

1. What are your thoughts on hearing from God?

2. Have you ever heard from God? If so, was it audible or more like a gut feeling?

3. What do you think are barriers to hearing more often from God?

Try a listening prayer. Allow yourself some time and quietness away from it all. Think of something small you want to ask God that you are genuinely unbiased about; something you could accept either way He chooses to answer. Focus on Jesus and welcome God's Holy Spirit. Focus on God and ask your question. It could be something like, "Who do you want me to pray for?" Thank Him that He is teaching you to have ears to hear Him. This may take several minutes, and you may have to meditate on God or Jesus for 10–20 minutes. Be patient, you may have a try a couple of times before He reveals His answer to you. Then just wait and experience this beautiful form of communication for yourself.

CHAPTER 9

Persistent Prayers

In Chapter 4, When God Doesn't Heal Right Away, I talked about how sometimes God is not saying no, He is saying not now. In the waiting, we must be persistent and patient. How many times have you heard, "Practice makes perfect," or "Try and try again"? The same applies to your prayers. Persistence is actually pleasing to God not annoying.

Elijah gives us a great example of this in the 1 Kings 18:43. In this story, there is a great drought in the land. After performing a great miracle that involved fire falling from the sky and consuming a waterlogged burnt offering, Elijah goes on to pray for rain. He climbed to the top of Mount Carmel and prayed. Then he told his servant to go and look towards the sea to see if there were any signs of rain. Unfortunately, there was nothing. But

Elijah knew about persistence. He told his servant to go back and check not once or twice, but seven times. Each time there was nothing to report. But on the seventh time his servant returned and said, "Behold a little cloud like a man's hand is rising from the sea." I don't know about you, but a tiny cloud as small as a fist does not make me think to grab my raincoat. However, that was all Elijah needed. He told his servant to go warn King Ahab, "Prepare your chariot and go down lest the rain stop you." It goes on to say, "And in a little while the heavens grew black with clouds and wind, and there was a great rain."

I wonder, if we knew God was going to answer our prayers on the seventh or the twenty seventh time, how might that change our prayer attitude? Would you keep asking with expectancy or would you give up and stop looking? Would any small progress fill you with hope and expectancy? In James 1:12 it states, "Blessed is the man who remains steadfast under trial, for when he has stood the test he will receive the crown of life, which God has promised to those who love him." God showed me the power of persistence recently when my husband was recovering from an ear surgery.

Last summer, my husband started complaining of pain in his left ear. Being a nurse, I used my otoscope to check his ears and noticed his eardrum was a little red but had a strange white area to the top right corner. I chalked it up to an ear infection and sent him to the doctors to get a prescription for antibiotics. They thought the same and prescribed him some antibiotics. He said it did not hurt terribly but felt like there was a lot of fluid inside. It did not improve, and his hearing declined as a ringing noise grew louder and louder. So, he went back to the doctors and they gave him a stronger antibiotic. He got worse and went back and they ordered a CT of his ear and an ENT referral. That ENT basically told him it was of no concern and he couldn't do anything about it. So, he made some phone calls to see a different ENT who took one look and said, "I don't think it's an infection or fluid. I think it is a cholesteatoma."

"A what," I said? I had never heard of such a thing. Basically, he had developed a benign tumor behind his eardrum. I thought to myself, here we go again!

The ENT said he needed another MRI and would schedule him with Dr. Michael, an ENT neurosurgeon, to remove it. I was glad we were persistent in finding another doctor. But we also had to be persistent in our prayers. The surgery itself was scary just because of the location. Nick's ear would have to be cut from behind and flapped open to expose the eardrum and hearing bones. The week before the surgery, the doctor told us he was hopeful that it was benign but there was a small chance that it could be malignant. He was certain Nick's ear bones would have to be replaced with prosthetic ear bones, but he was not sure if the mastoid or jawbone was also affected. He was also concerned that Nick's hearing nerve could be in a precarious situation as well. There was a lot of, "what ifs." We are usually pretty private and don't like to ask for help or prayers, but on this prayer journey, I decided it was the right thing to do. So, we asked our life group at church, as well as our friends and family, to pray for Nick's upcoming surgery. Nick's parents came with us on the one hour drive to the northside of the city on the day of surgery. We prayed again for him before and during surgery. Finally, Dr. Michael came to the waiting room to update us that he had successfully removed all of the tumor and, thank the Lord, it was indeed benign and fully encapsulated.

The surgery was a success, but the road to recovery was just beginning. During the first week Nick couldn't even open his mouth to speak, he wrote everything down on a whiteboard. But slowly healing began. Nick would have loved to be all healed up in two weeks and tell you his hearing was fully restored, and the loud ringing went away. However, God again doesn't always operate on our timetable. I made it a habit of praying for Nick and the healing and restoration of his ear every morning. He had monthly checkups with the ENT for four months. Each time his hearing improved by about 10 decibels. There were days and moments when the ringing stopped or quieted down and he had some long-awaited peace, but then it would return.

By about the fourth month, we had adjusted, and life was getting back to normal. For some reason, I had stopped praying for Nick's ear. I thought he had healed as much as he was going to. Then he started complaining more about the ringing and asked, "Have you stopped praying for my ear?" I was a little surprised and said, "Actually I have, why?" He said, "Because I can tell." When you were praying for my ear, it felt better and now that you have stopped it is worse. I was kind of shocked, after about 100 days of praying, I felt like my prayers weren't really doing any good anymore. So, I had moved on to praying for other things in our busy lives. Has this ever happened to you? Have you ever given up on something or moved on thinking you were not making any progress? In 1 Thessalonians 5:16, it says, "Rejoice always, **pray without ceasing**, **give thanks** in all circumstances; for this is the will of God in Christ Jesus for you." In Psalms 35:28, David says, "Then my tongue shall tell of your righteousness and of your praise **all the day long**."

The next checkup was about six months after the surgery and there was a watch spot. It was a concave circular area that was not healing right on his eardrum. The ENT was considering another procedure, but he wanted to just watch it for now. I continued to pray every day.

"Jesus, thank you that you are restoring health and wholeness into my husband's ear. Thank you that his eardrum is strengthening. Thank you that his eustachian tube is remaining open." While I prayed, I envisioned the tissues healing.

At the one-year checkup the ENT had changed his mind and was against the surgery and the procedure stating it was looking slightly better. At the two-year checkup, he watch spot was gone and even in the proper convex shape. When my husband told me the good report, I gave thanks and praise to God that He can do all things even better than I could ever imagine!

In Luke 18, you can read about the parable of the persistent widow. In this short parable, a widow seeks justice against her adversary from an atheist judge who doesn't have any respect for others. At first, the judge denied the widow, but she kept coming back seeking justice anyway. After a while, this judge finally gave in because he didn't want to be bothered anymore. The point of the parable is if an atheist judge will give in and provide justice, how much more will a loving heavenly Father provide justice to his children who are persistent? Jesus is encouraging us to pray persistently in Luke 18:1, "And he told them a parable to the effect that they ought always to pray and not lose heart."

Discussion Questions:

1. What are some things that seem impossible for you to fix or overcome in your own strength?

2. Have you given up on certain hopes or dreams?

3. Have you ever prayed persistently? If so, what were the outcomes?

Pray that you can surrender the impossible things you can't seem to do in your own strength. Thank God daily that He is willing and able to do those impossible things in your life. Declare He is working all things for your good and His glory. Visualize those possibilities when you are praying. Don't give up; keep praying every day and see what happens.

Prayer Example
Use the lines below to write out a prayer you want to pray daily for something you have not been able to fix in your own strength.

_____

_____

_____

CHAPTER 10

Roadblocks

Forgiveness

In the Lord's Prayer, Jesus states, "And forgive us our sins; for we also forgive every one that is indebted to us." Sometimes, our prayer connection to God is blocked because of unforgiveness in our own hearts. In Mark 11:20, Peter had just noticed that the fig tree Jesus had cursed has now withered, and Jesus goes on to tell them about the power of faith combined with forgiveness. Jesus states, "Have faith in God. Truly, I say to you, whoever says to this mountain, 'Be taken up and thrown into the sea,' and does not doubt in his heart, but believes that what he says will come to pass, it will be done for him. Therefore, I tell you, whatever you ask in prayer, believe that you have received it, and it will be yours. And *when you stand praying,* forgive, if you have anything against anyone, so that your Father also who is in heaven may forgive you your trespasses." Some say that Abraham's beloved son Joseph was blessed with so much because he forgave so much. I truly believe that faith activates prayers, but forgiveness can really allow for more of God's Holy Spirit to flow through you. However, this can be one of those things that is easier said than done, especially if someone you love has deeply hurt you.

The good news is that you do not have to do it alone. If you are having trouble forgiving someone, you can ask your heavenly Father to help you forgive them. Yes, that's right you can just ask your heavenly Father. It is really just that simple. I had to ask God to help me forgive an unfair boss and family members when I just could not do it on my own, and He did! Remember, in the end, the forgiveness is not really for the other person who wronged you. Dear friend, forgiveness is for you! Hanging on to all that hate and resentment only consumes and hurts you. While you spend all night tossing and turning thinking about how the other person wronged you, the other person is most likely sleeping like a baby. Another helpful thing to remember is we are all sinners in need of a savior. Jesus says we must forgive others, so we can be forgiven of our own sins and trespasses. This one truth helped me to forgive my own grandfather from the hurtful things he said and did to our family.

It was a warm summer morning when the phone rang just as I was heading out the door. I answered it and to my surprise it was my crazy aunt who we will call Janice. Maybe you have one of those relatives in your family too. There always seems to be one in most families. Some might even claim their family put the funk in dysfunction. Anyway, I had not spoken to my aunt in over seven years due to her drug problems. She didn't call to say good morning or wish me well. She started right in with hurtful false accusations threatening me. In my professional experience, I have found there is really no point in arguing with a drug addict. So, I hung up the phone.

To make a very long story short, my grandfather basically turned his two daughters against one another after becoming addicted to prescription narcotics himself. He made really poor choices while taking those drugs that caused a few car accidents. Unfortunately, he had every legal right to make those poor choices. After the lawyers settled everything, our family was left divided. I learned that my grandfather really was not the man I thought he once was. He even went along with my aunt's false accusations against my own mother and myself. It reminded me of a scene from the movie *The Lord of the Rings*, where the old King Théoden of Rohan was brainwashed by an evil advisor Grima Wormtongue. I felt kind of like the princess, stuck with a father who looked like her father and dressed like her father, yet his mind was lost to evil. That is what drugs will do to a family. I was left hurt and in shock, I still just don't understand how any good father could do that to his own family. It was certainly not acceptable for my own household. Despite the pain somewhere deep down inside, I just knew everything was happening for a reason, and God would even use this tragedy for good. I just did not know what it was, but the thought still gave me some comfort. It was hard, but I think that is what it means to trust in the Lord, even when it hurts and doesn't look like it would ever be right again.

I tried to forgive my grandfather on my own, but try as I might, I just couldn't. I would lay awake at night thinking about it. I found myself unable to focus during the day. I knew that I should forgive him, but I just did not know how. I was so full of anger and pain. So, I turned it over to God and prayed for Him to help me forgive my grandfather. Then one cool crisp autumn afternoon, it hit me while I was out taking our collie for a walk through the neighborhood. I am a sinner, and if Jesus can forgive me then He can forgive my grandfather too. It wasn't a full recovery, but it was enough to bring some peace to my soul. That simple truth helped me to start taking small steps towards more and more forgiveness. In order to fully forgive, I had to start looking past my grandfather's sins and try to see some goodness. Then I would need to reach the hardest part, being able to offer mercy and grace the same way Jesus offered it to me.

Next, I confessed my struggle of unforgiveness to one of our youth pastors who also struggled with this when his mother passed away from a drug overdose. He shared some of the truths that helped him overcome the hurt and then prayed with me. We asked God again to help heal the hurt and boldly asked God to remove the drug addiction. Soon I was able to pray prayers like, "Thank you for helping me to forgive my grandfather. In the name of Jesus Christ, he is now forgiven. Amen." The next step took a little more time for me. But now I am at a point where I pray for God to help him and even bless my grandfather in the name of Jesus. I pray one day they will be free from their prescription drug addictions and my family will be restored again. But until then, I will remember them the way they used to be before the drugs and pray they will be able to overcome their temptations and addictions.

A friend of ours personally experienced healing from prayer combined with forgiveness. Back in his early twenties, our friend, who we will call Kevin, was in college when he started having back pain. Then he experienced loss of mobility; he could no longer bend down and touch his toes. It became impossible to play sports. Over the Christmas break, he went to the orthopedic doctor and to his surprise was diagnosed with a herniated disc in his lower back. The doctor said it was pretty bad and would require surgery coupled with a lengthy recovery period. He went on to recommend steroid shots over spring break and scheduled the surgery during summer break to allow for several weeks of healing.

Spring break came and he received his steroid shots. Then, about a month later at his church's men's group, they decided to pray for him one Saturday evening; there were about seven or eight men in the group. They all gathered around Kevin and laid hands on him. They prayed for the healing and restoration of his back. After the prayer, one of the guys came up to him and said, "I just have this feeling you are going to be feeling better tomorrow morning." Kevin thanked him but didn't really think much else of it.

The next day was Sunday and he went to Church as usual. But during the service something unexpected happened. The preacher looked around the room and said, "There are three men here with back pain who are going to be healed today. I don't know who they are, but they need to first forgive someone who has wronged them." Now, as far as he knew, the preacher did not know about Kevin's medical condition and did not even really know Kevin on a personal level at all. Kevin knew instantly that this message was for him. He also knew instantly the person he needed to forgive was his own father. So, right then and there, he prayed to God and out loud forgave his father. Then instantly he suddenly felt a warm sensation all throughout his chest and torso. Kevin recalls, "I mean I was so warm, sweat was actually pouring off me." Afterwards he did feel better. Additionally, he felt that an emotional burden had been lifted from him.

Several weeks passed and, before he knew it, it was time to see the doctor again to schedule his surgery. The doctor examined him and was astonished at how well he was. Kevin said, "That steroid shot was great, afterwards I really haven't had any more pain." The doctor replied, "That was seven weeks ago, and those steroid shots only last a week or so. I don't know how but you are healed, and I can't ethically perform surgery on you now. There is nothing wrong with you." Kevin was in awe; the doctor had just confirmed God's healing.

When it comes to healing prayers, unforgiveness can truly block our connection to receive more of God's healing Holy Spirit. Additionally, forgiveness may be the greater gift than our own wants and desires of an earthly healing. In Mark 2:5, it reads, "And when Jesus saw their faith, he said to the paralytic, 'Son, your sins are forgiven.'" Did you catch that, Jesus did not say you are healed, he said your sins are forgiven? Jesus did go on to heal the paralytic to bring glory to the Father, but first he forgave him. True forgiveness is a deep act of kindness that can be a powerful healing. However, true forgiveness can be hard to achieve on your own, especially if you are filled with anger or grief. If you find that you are struggling to forgive someone in your life, try asking God to help you forgive them. Then when you are ready, it is really just as simple as proclaiming they are forgiven to God. And don't forget to check the mirror, sometimes the person we need to forgive is ourselves.

Confessing Our Own Sins

James 5:16 states, "Therefore, confess your sins to one another and pray for one another, that you may be healed. The prayer of the righteous person has great power as it is working." There it is, if you want your healing prayer to have great power, confess your sins to one another and pray for each other. If your church has a confessional this may be easy for you. However, if your church does not, you can still do this. I decided to try this just recently. As a matter a fact, this year I decided I was taking Lent to another level. I was not going to give up bread or chocolate, but instead I was going to give up unforgiveness and confess my sins. Yes, that's right. But who to forgive first, I wondered? Ah yes, let's start with me. To do that I would need to list all my sins.

The wise Agnes Sanford, author of *The Healing Light*, suggests a method she found profoundly helpful. The first step was to divide my life into seven sections. Then each day, I would pray and meditate on that section of my life. Thinking back to the uncomfortable memories that made me feel guilty, I wrote down my sins and any resentments I had of others during that section of my life. By the end of seven days, I had written a lengthy list of sins I had long forgotten. I prayed out loud thanking God for forgiving me of my sins. It was very freeing and unusually satisfying. It reminded me of the feeling I get right after I clean out my closet. You know that feeling when you get rid of all that junk you haven't worn in years, but haven't taken the time to toss out?

Fears and Doubt

As my husband and I were driving down the road one warm summer day, we passed a sign that said, "Feed your faith and your fears will starve to death." If you think about it, it goes both ways. Feed your fears and your faith will starve to death.

Sometimes it is our own fears and doubts that block God's provision in our lives. In Matthew 14, Peter sees a ghost-like figure walking on water in the middle of the night walking towards them. The disciples cried out in fear. Jesus says to them, "Take heart, it is I. Do not be afraid." Peter does something unexpected. He says to Jesus, "Lord, if it is you, command me to come to you on the water." Jesus replies, "Come." Peter gets out of the boat and walks on the water to Jesus. But when Peter took his eyes off Jesus and focused on the strong winds, he became afraid and began to sink. Peter cried out to Jesus, "Lord, save me." Jesus reached out his hand and took hold of him saying, "Oh you of little faith, why did you doubt?" In James 1:6, it states, "But let him ask in faith, with no doubting, for the one who doubts is like a wave of the sea that is driven and tossed by the wind.

Is fear and doubt holding you back from the God-sized dreams He has placed in your heart? Is your faith growing or is your fear? You can have comfort or growth, but not both. Which will you choose?

Disobedience
When we obey the promptings of the Holy Spirit and the calling God has for us, unexpected blessings usually follow. Many times, God asks us to step out of our comfort zones and listen to the

guidance of the Holy Spirit. It may not always make logical sense. You might feel a calling to forgive, help, feed, pray, love, or give to someone. The calling usually aligns with the fruits of the Holy Spirit mentioned in Galatians 5:22. These include love, joy, peace, patience, kindness, goodness, faithfulness, gentleness, and self-control.

A small-scale example occurred on my way to a parent-teacher conference. I had to stop by the grocery store on the way. While I was there, I had this strange urge to buy Reese's Peanut Butter Cups to give to my son's teacher during our meeting. I wasn't sure why, but I decided to buy them and brought them to the meeting with me. Before I got out of the car, I felt a little silly following this urge to buy her candy and questioned it for a second. "What if she doesn't even like Reese's cups?" Then I decided to do it anyway. Not thinking much of it, I greeted her and gave her the candy. I had never seen someone so grateful for Reese's cups! She asked if I wouldn't mind if she went ahead and ate them right there in front of me. She explained how she hadn't gotten a chance to eat lunch that day and was starving. Now I wished I had bought her something more. I was glad I chose to obey the prompting of the Holy Spirit. When we obey God, He can use us to help others and bring glory and honor to Him. When you flip the scenario and disobey, we miss out on God's best intent and experience for us. There is great power in obedience. However, this great power is blocked when we disobey. It is like a sin by omission.

If you think that you have disobeyed, do not be discouraged. We serve a patient and long-suffering Father. Just simply pray and ask God to show you any areas you have disobeyed. Then ask for His forgiveness. Ask Him to give you strength and courage to help you obey the future promptings and callings He has for your life.

Distractions

I think another big roadblock is when we can't focus on God because we are too distracted. What are you making time for in your daily life? There are a lot of distractions that look interesting, fun, and appealing but in the end rob us of our time, joy, peace, and rest. What are you saying yes to that forces you to have to say no to what God is calling you to? The problem with distractions is they can be subtle. For me, I am easily distracted. I can set off to go to the kitchen and walk past the laundry and start putting away clothes and forget what I was looking for in the kitchen. Emails, social media, and my phone are also great distractions. So, it is important to try to focus and schedule time to spend with God in prayer and reading his word. Make it a priority. I do find that when I start my day with his word or in prayer, my whole day seems to be smoother than the days that I forget or don't make time for it. We might easily say I just don't have time to read or pray, but if we take a look at our average daily screen time, we might find some extra lost time. Pastor Mark Driscoll poses the question, "are we trading our fruitfulness for business?

My husband and I were listening to one of Dave Ramsey's audiobooks on retirement and in it Dave described a great visual lesson that stuck with me. The lesson was simple; it began with a large glass vase. If you fill it to the top with large rocks, is it full? What if you poured in tiny pebbles next? Is it full now? What if you poured in sand next? Is it full now? What if you poured in water next? Now it is full. What can we learn from this demonstration? The vase represents time. The lesson is simple. If you don't plan the big important things first, all the little things will come in and steal your time and fill up your days. Satan would love for you to get distracted from what God has for you. What are you pursuing? Ask yourself, "Is what I'm doing God's will for me?"

Discussion Questions

1. What are some roadblocks in your own prayer life?

2. When was the last time you confessed your sins?

3. What can you do to make time for God?

Pray that God would reveal any prayer roadblocks to you and thank Him for His forgiveness, mercy, and love.

Prayer Example

Merciful God, you heal and restore health by the powerful presence of your Holy Spirit. Thank you that you forgive and restore what is broken. Father, I repent of my sins. Help us to see past the lies of our sins and guide us back to your truth and righteousness. Help me to forgive so that I may also be forgiven. Reveal any unknown sins or roadblocks that need forgiveness. Thank you that your grace, love, and mercy abound so that we can claim the freedom that you offer from sin and un-forgiveness. Protect us from the distractions and temptations of this life. This we pray in your Son's holy precious and powerful name. Amen.

CHAPTER 11

Scientific Evidence

Many medical professionals tend to shy away from prayer and only address the physical or mental needs of their patients. I suspect that might be because the science and research surrounding prayer is rarely discussed or studied. To be clear, I would never suggest ignoring the science of medicine and solely focus on prayer. I am simply saying there are some amazing possibilities when you add God and prayer to the equation. I once read a sign as I entered a very old Catholic hospital that simply put it this way, "We dress the wound, God does the healing."

Take a look at one of the greatest medical centers in the world, the Mayo Clinic in Minnesota. It was founded and directed by an incredible physician who was an entrepreneur of his time.

However, the idea and funding for the Mayo Clinic came in a vision received by Mother Alfred of the order of the Sisters of St. Francis. In this vision, God told Mother Alfred to build a hospital with Dr. Mayo and his sons and it would become world-renowned for its art of medicine. The hospital would be open to all people. No one would have guessed such a partnership would spring out of the middle of nowhere. In 1889, St. Mary's Hospital was built, and it became known as the miracle in the corn field (Burns, Ewers, and Ewers 2018). Today the Mayo Clinic has kept its founding principles of faith, hope, and science. Is the success of the Mayo Clinic coincidental or is there something powerful when we partner the science of medicine with our faith in God?

Another great example of this amazing partnership of science and prayer is seen in the remarkable neurosurgeon Dr. Ben Carson. He has performed miraculous surgeries that other doctors around the world have deemed impossible. Even Dr. Carson does not lay claim to all of the glory for his gifted hands. In his book *Gifted Hands*, Dr. Carson explains how he always assigns homework for the parents of the child he is about to operate on. He tells them, "Say your prayers, I really think it does help." He goes on to say, "I always tell parents that because I believe it myself. I've not had anybody disagree with me." Is it coincidental that

Dr. Ben Carson is able to do the impossible and have parents praying over the surgery?

Before we dive into the how, let's examine the why. Afterall, "An education of the mind without the education of the heart is no education at all,"- Aristotle. Why should we pray? What does God get out of it when we pray? Some would say praying creates an opportunity for miracles to occur. In Dr. Craig Keener's exhaustive two-volume reference book, *Miracles,* he uncovers hundreds of modern-day miracles all over the world backed by solid observable evidence (Keener 2011). What can be noted throughout his research is that prayer occurred each time prior to the miraculous healing. To answer the question why would God use prayer and miracles to heal, Keener states, "They show us his power, but also his benevolence and compassion. (Strobel, 2018)." What effect does a miraculous healing have on a person or group of people? Dr. Craig Keener states in his interview with Lee Strobel that, "Some estimate that 90 percent of the church in China is being fueled by healings (Strobel 2018)." He went on to list several other countries where miraculous healings were directly correlated with the growth of the Christian church (Strobel 2018). If you think about it, healing is one of God's primary tools to demonstrate who He is and rapidly grow his church.

Now that we have investigated the why, let us dive into the science of praying. In grade school science we learned about the laws of nature. These include the invisible laws that have a visible effect such as gravity and electromagnetism. Take a moment and look all around you. You can't see it but there is electricity in the atmosphere all around you. There are magnetic fields all around you as well. You may remember learning about this wonderful invisible energy called electricity that flows all around us in the atmosphere, producing visible lightning. In the same way, your spirit and the Holy Spirit are invisible but can produce very visible effects.

In medical or nursing school we learned that electrical currents even flow through our bodies and cause our hearts to beat. We can see their effects every time we connect a patient to a heart monitor or as we read electrocardiograms (EKGs). In Anatomy & Physiology class, we learned that this electricity powers our incredible nervous system allowing us to think, move, and feel. A fun way to physically see this human electricity at home is to purchase a $5.00 energy ball that lights up and makes a sound when two or more people touch it and hold hands in a circle. Additionally, there are magnetic fields all throughout the earth and inside our bodies. Tiny electromagnetic fields in every single proton in our bodies are what allow magnetic resonance imaging or MRIs to see our internal organs. Through these laws of nature, scientists learn how to interact and connect to the elements and powers in and all around us.

If God created power within the laws of nature, how does His power seem to disregard them? Although most miraculous healings appear to defy the laws of nature, often they actually work within the laws of nature (Sanford 2013). In an interview with Dr. Craig Keener, author of *The Historical Jesus of the Gospels* and *Miracles, he* gives a simple demonstration of this point using the law of gravity (Strobel 2018). He takes his pen and states, "If I drop this pen, the law of gravity tells me it will fall to the floor. But if I were to reach in and grab the pen in midair, I wouldn't be violating the law of gravity; I would merely be intervening. And certainly, if God exists, He will have the ability to intervene in the world that He himself created (Strobel 2018)."

The energy and powers of God are similar to the energy and powers defined in the laws of nature. His invisible power is all around you, and even in you, but sometimes the conditions are not right to allow you to see or feel His power. Similarly, in biology we learned how important conditions are. For example, plants can only grow if the conditions are right. You must have the right soil, water, temperature, and sunlight. If you take any of these conditions away, then the plant will die. Similarly, with prayer there are conditions that improve the growth and healing of your prayers. Some conditions that improve prayer include having your heart in the right place, aligning with God's will, belief, and being free of the roadblocks discussed in the previous chapter.

If you have ever bought a new house, you always make sure to call up the local electric company to ensure your house has access to the wonderful power of electricity before or on moving day. If you fail to do so, no matter how many times you flip the light switch, the lights will not turn on. The conditions are not right for you to experience the power of electricity. In order for you to make your lights turn on, you must first seek out the electrical company, contact them, and set your house up to receive this electricity. Then you can plug in your lamp and turn it on to see and experience the power of electricity.

God's power works very similarly, first you must seek and connect with Him. Then simply welcome and receive God's powerful Holy Spirit in you. Turn it on with faith and thanksgiving to experience the power of God. Then you are ready to connect the power of the Holy Spirit to the patient by laying hands on them. Jesus demonstrates this laying on of hands for us in Luke 4:40, "Now when the sun was setting, all those who were sick with various diseases brought them to him, and he laid his hands on every one of them and healed them." Then just be still and know He is God. Other effective elements of prayer include multiple people praying and being persistent. God often likes to wait for the just the right moment, when all hope seems lost to show up and show out. I think He does this to prove to us without a shadow of a doubt that it was God and not anything else.

Maybe that sounds too simple and you are looking for more evidence-based research. Let's consider the study published in the 1999 *Archives of Internal Medicine Journal* by Dr. William S. Harris "A Randomized, Controlled Trial of the Effects of Remote, Intercessory Prayer on Outcomes in Patients Admitted to the Coronary Care Unit." In this random double-blind study of 1,013 admitted coronary patients, approximately half were unknowingly assigned a Christian to pray for them daily and approximately half were not (Harris et al. 1999). The results concluded that the patients who were prayed for had less complications and better outcomes than those who did not (Harris et al. 1999). What can we learn from this study about prayer? Remote intercessory prayer is better than no prayer.

Let's take it a step further and consider the study published in *Southern Medical Journal* by

Dale Matthew in 2001, "Effects of Intercessory Prayer on Patients with Rheumatoid Arthritis." He studied 40 patients with diagnosed rheumatoid arthritis (Matthews, Marlowe, and McNutt 2001). In his study, 19 randomly selected patients received daily intercessory prayer for healing remotely and the other 21 received daily in-person prayer over a period of 6 months (Matthews, Marlowe, and McNutt 2001). At the one-year follow-up, guess who showed significant health improvements using 10 specific variables? As you might have guessed, it was those who received in-person prayer daily for 6 months (Matthews, Marlowe, and McNutt 2001). From this study, two elements of effective prayer are discovered. Being physically present and close to the patient and being persistent have shown a better outcome.

If you think about it, it is not really that complicated. God can intervene in the very laws of nature that He created. You are simply connecting yourself with the power of God's Holy Spirit and then connecting that power and energy with your patient. To review:

1. Connect by welcoming God's Holy Spirit.
2. Activate your prayer with faith and thanksgiving.
3. Lay your hands on the patient.
4. Allow God to work through you.

Discussion Questions

1. How has prayer and healing grown your own faith or those around you?

2. Have you ever seen God show up when all seemed lost?

3. Why do you think God uses healing to grow his church?

Purchase a low-cost energy ball and follow the experiment instructions to see the power of the electrical currents in our bodies.

Thank God that He is helping to grow your understanding of the hows and the whys of prayer.

Prayer Example
God of all creation, all life in this great universe is your handiwork. Thank you for growing us in wisdom and understanding of how and why you work through prayer. Let us experience more of the Holy Spirit to see and feel the visible effects of your invisible power. Through your love we draw our strength. Let our prayers be pleasing to you and bring forth your glory and honor. We pray all this in your son Jesus's holy and precious name. Amen.

CHAPTER 12

When God Calls Us Home

Sometimes God is not going to answer our prayers for healing, not because He doesn't care or because He doesn't want what is best for us. It might be because He is calling us home to Him instead. There in heaven, He will restore all health and wholeness with an eternal everlasting body. God has predetermined the number of each person's life. In Psalms 139:16, King David proclaims, "Your eyes saw my unformed substance; in your book were written, every one of them, the days that were formed for me." Job 14:5–7 states, "Since his days are determined, and the number of his months is with you and you have appointed his limits that he cannot pass." God is going to fulfill the number of the days He has given us, even when His timetable doesn't align with ours. Despite our prayers for an earthly healing, sometimes God uses heavenly healing instead. Other times God is not ready to call you home, and no illness can take you despite the odds. A dear nursing friend of mine, who we will call Marie, witnessed this in an unusual way.

One afternoon, Marie called me up to tell me how three weeks ago, a seventy-two-year-old woman entered their ER in an unstable junctional escape heart rhythm. Her heart was beating at an extremely slow rate of just 28 beats per minute. The normal heart rate is 60–100 beats per minute. "We tried everything; she didn't respond to the atropine, and we even tried pacing her, but we couldn't obtain capture," she explained. Epinephrine was the only drug she responded to. A Life Flight helicopter was called to transport her to a larger facility. Then five minutes before they arrived her heart stopped, and they began CPR. They were able to restart her heart and get a pulse momentarily before she went into cardiac arrest four more times! By that time, the helicopter team was waiting and deemed her too unstable to transport by air. When they finally got her heart restarted for the fifth time, they had to transport her by ground ambulance service. On the way to the other hospital, she died one more time in the back of the ambulance. They performed CPR and got her heart restarted yet again. My friend was unsure of her outcome after that. What she did know was this was the kind of woman who never met a stranger. Every week in church, she would make sure to smile and welcome each and every person she saw. The ED team prayed for her that day.

Fast forward to yesterday, the Emergency Department manager of that same ED received word that one of their ER nurses, one of the sweetest, most caring people you'd ever meet, was found passed away in her bed that morning. She had died in her sleep at the young age of 48. She was a devout Catholic woman with eight children. She was a true angel among us.

The whole ED team was devastated. As my friend walked in the hospital that morning at 7 a.m., their doctor, the ED staff, hospital staff, and the housekeeping team got together. They gave a group hug and prayed for each other and for her family. They told each other how much they loved each other and had a good cry. "We just don't know what we will do without her," Marie confessed through tears. She was not just an incredible asset to our hospital, but an angel to all her patients. As an ED nurse, she even found hospice care for one of our nursing home residents during her ER visit. She stayed with the woman holding her hand as she passed from this world to the next.

Then at 10:30 a.m., the day after their beloved colleague passed away, a miracle happened. That adorable little old lady who died six times, three weeks ago, walked into the hospital. That's right, she got right out of her car accompanied by her son and husband. She checked-in for her rehabilitation appointment. Marie went to the vending machine and couldn't believe her eyes. There she was, alive and well! Marie introduced herself and the patient went on to share her story. She told Marie that when she died, she saw her dead relatives and they told her she had to go back now; it wasn't time because her name wasn't on the list yet! So even though she died six times that day, it simply was not her time to die. She looked great; she had no deficits at all. Her only complaint was some chest soreness from all of the CPR compressions.

My friend Marie writes:

> "In this time of sorrow, we have been blessed with a miracle. God is with us! As we all process this, we learn that one thing is for certain. 'Man's days are determined; you (God) have decreed the number of his months and have set limits he

cannot exceed' (Job 14:5). Every day is a gift we shall not take for granted."

We witnessed another miracle when my husband's uncle, Joe, went to be with the Lord last summer. It was an early Friday morning at the hospice care home. Nurse Judy was checking on her patients. She entered Joe's room when she saw it. It made her smile, and she went on about her rounds. A little later that Friday morning my father-in-law, Todd, had finally arrived to remain by his dying brother's bedside. All morning Joe was seeing and talking to people who no one else could see in the room. He would smile and laugh and say things like, "You're funny. You're a funny guy. I got to go now." Finally, all his family had finally arrived and gathered around him on the left side of his bed. His brother Todd noticed that Joe would keep glancing back at the right corner of the room. He would look at his family on his left side when they spoke to him, but then his gaze would return back to the right corner of the room. His brother Todd thought maybe he was just more comfortable looking in that direction. As a medical professional, this right sided gaze could easily be chalked up to a possible neurological deficit possibly related to inadequate blood flow and perfusion to Joe's brain. However, he was able to look to the left when he responded to those in the room.

The family took turns sharing memories and saying their goodbyes. Then Gladys, the preacher, came. She spoke a beautiful prayer over Joe. When she finished, she told Joe in a soothing voice, it was okay, he could let go now. Even after all his family had said their goodbyes, he was still struggling like he was still trying to stay for some reason. Joe was painfully forcing each breath. Gladys asked, "Is there anyone he would be waiting for?"

"Well," confessed Todd, "the only one that is not here is our brother Tony." So, they decided to call Tony and put him on speaker phone. The phone rang and Tony's wife, Jessica, answered. She and Tony said their goodbyes to Joe. They told him that they loved him, and it was okay if he needed to go. It was within minutes of that phone call that Joe stopped fighting for each breath. You could see the relief wash over him. Then, within just a few minutes, just like that, he was gone. His body became still, and his soul departed. The family stayed and kept each other company that afternoon in the hospice home.

Todd went outside to get some fresh air. As he glanced up at the crisp blue sky, his gaze fell upon the hospice house and he noticed his wife through the kitchen window. He decided to go back inside through the porch. As he entered the house, he ran into Nurse Judy again. She gave Todd a warm smile and said, "When I came to see Joe early in morning, I saw it." Todd asked curiously, "Saw what?"

"I saw the glow of heaven up in that corner," Nurse Judy answered. Todd pointed to the right corner of the room, and said, "That corner?" She smiled and said yes. Todd said, "That is where Joe kept looking. His focus would always go back to that corner. That is where he was looking when he was talking to the people who were not physically there." The nurse confessed, "Every now and then I have seen the glow of heaven when people pass from this world to the next, but not all of the time." Todd smiled back at Nurse Judy as tears of joy started to well up. This really brought Todd and the rest of the family comfort. Believe it or not, Joe had lived a pretty rough life and made a lot of poor choices. However, he did believe in God. He had been baptized when he was little. Just a couple years ago as Joe's liver began to fail, his brother Al had led Joe to pray the sinner's prayer with him.

Sometimes during the transition from this world to the next, you can also feel a warmth, peace, and comfort that one hospice nurse describes as a "God hug." Last week, a hospice nurse friend, Mary, wrote and shared her experience with a 49-year-old man named Matt. Matt was diagnosed with terminal brain cancer. She had been caring for Matt daily for about three weeks now. Matt was a wildly restless patient, but Mary had this strange connection with him from the moment their eyes met.

Matt had lived a rough life of drugs and alcohol, but he was a talented motorcycle mechanic. Mary said, "It was hard to explain, but it seemed as if he was fighting demons on the inside." Mary decided to silently pray for him daily. Last Saturday, his caregivers called Mary frantically. She got in her car and rushed over. She arrived to find Matt naked; he had pulled out the Huber needle from his port and his Foley catheter from his bladder. With his eyes closed tightly, he seemed confused and angry. Mary remained calm; she knew Matt could understand her. So, she asked Matt, "Open your eyes and look at my eyes." He slowly opened them. Mary's clear blue eyes held him with a steady, uncompromising gaze. Then she smiled and teased, "Yours are bluer than mine," and asked him gently to settle down. Amazingly he calmed right down as she began caring for him and gave him his medications. "It was amazing to watch Matt enter a state of absolute peace."

The following Thursday, Mary was hustling to see patients and, at the last second, she had this prompting gut instinct telling her to go see Matt earlier in the day instead of in the afternoon.

When she arrived, Matt was calm. Mary was not able to get a blood pressure and all of Matt's family had said their goodbyes. His heart rate had been in the low 40s all night and he was breathing easy. The family was stumped about one thing Matt had said last night. They explained to Mary, Matt said he was "fighting with Peter and Paul to enter Heaven." Mary went over to Matt and touched his hand, she silently prayed over Matt and then whispered, "Hi, Matt, it is Mary. You're all calm now and I'm so thankful." As she held Matt's hand, one lone tear rolled from his right eye and then he was gone. As he left this world, Mary could feel a soft electricity from his hand, and it covered her in an absolute peace. "Well, it was just so beautiful," she explained. "I knew in that moment he was carried home by an angel, I could feel it. To think that someone who many would say was not God's child was now in His arms. I am 100% sure he is in Heaven. It was a God hug." Mary had been there for only seven minutes before Matt transitioned into the next world.

These true stories are not always well publicized, but just ask an experienced hospice nurse. You may find that he or she has seen the glow of heaven, felt a God hug, or even witnessed a miracle as their patient was called home to heaven. I have read about others who have seen the glow of heaven. If you look for them, you can find these beautiful true stories.

As I was finishing up this book, my husband confessed he too saw a strange glowing light early one morning. It was at 6 a.m. just after the alarm had gone off. He went on to explain:

> "The alarm clock had just gone off and I rolled over to turn off the alarm. Realizing I didn't have to wake up early that day, I rolled back over to rest longer. As I rolled over to face you, I was blinded by a bright light. I thought maybe a car's headlights were shining in through our bedroom window. The strange thing was when I opened my eyes, it was pitch black. But, as soon as I closed my eyes again there was this blinding bright light all around you. It was so bright, I had to roll over the other way with my back towards you to get some rest. I knew just then that God was with you and blessing your work on this book."

My eyes were wide open in disbelief. I went on to explain to him what I was actually doing after the alarm went off that morning. After I heard the alarm go off at 6 a.m., I decided to pray before I got out of bed. It is sort of a habit I have created. Every morning before my feet hit the ground, I like to surrender the day to God, invite the Holy Spirit in, and then pray for everyone I can think of. That particular morning, my kids had final exams and I didn't have to take them so early. This meant I had lots of extra time to pray. As a matter a fact, when I finally said amen and got up and looked at the alarm clock it was 6:30 a.m. I was praying for about 30 minutes. I was praying for my husband, my children, my family, and, in particular, I was lifting up my nursing friend's husband, Mike, who had badly burned his hand from a blowtorch at work the night before.

I didn't get to see any blinding bright lights or really even feel anything unusual. But, what an incredible gift for my husband to be able to see a glimpse of God's Holy Spirit at work when we pray. It was just the encouragement I needed that day to keep on praying and finish up this book that God had put in my heart to write. That afternoon, my friend Susanna texted me and told me that her husband's hand was drastically better, with decreased swelling and restored blood flow.

I pray as you finish reading this book that you will be forever encouraged to keep praying. God is working through our prayers even when we can't see it.

Discussion Questions

1. Have you ever read about or heard someone share their near-death experience?

2. What are your thoughts about death and the transition from this body in this world to the unseen spiritual realm?

3. Have you ever requested a moment of silence to pray following a death pronouncement of a patient in your hospital? If not, give it a try.

Pray that God's Holy Spirit would be a guide to you as you help your patients or loved one's transition from this world to the next.

Prayer Example
(Following an unexpected death) Eternal and merciful God, we are gathered around the deathbed of our beloved friend and relative _____. Father, we ask that your Holy Spirit guide our words as we face the reality of this painful unexpected loss. Draw us nearer to you and to each other. Father, we surrender and commend _____'s spirit into your loving arms. We imagine his/her family and ancestors there to welcome him/her to be with you and the saints. May you provide _____'s family with the peace and comfort of

the Holy Spirit who abides in us always. We cling to your promises that all who believed in you would never know the sting of death but be raised to eternal and everlasting life forever. In Jesus's holy, precious, and powerful name, we pray all these things. Amen.

Conclusion

When I first embarked on this spiritual journey, I had no idea of the impact it would have on my life and the lives of those around me. As this journey comes to an end, we find ourselves back at the beginning. If we go back to our roots, we discover the missing piece of the puzzle, the truth that was somehow omitted from all of our training and education. We unveiled something so profound and deeper than just the physical. The way we were meant to care for others holistically is revealed, including not just the mind and the body, but also the soul. The solution is truly as simple as adding prayer to our interventions.

From the time I first began writing this book, until I typed these last sentences, my goal has been to share what God has revealed about prayer through scripture and real-life testimonies. May these truths help you connect back to your purpose and equip you to pray in ways you never thought possible. Even with his last breath on the cross Jesus used it to pray aloud. I challenge you to invite prayer into your daily plan of care for your patients and loved ones and experience this deeper healing for yourselves. May God bless you with courage, wisdom, health, strength, love, and compassion. May His light shine through you and bring healing to all those in need.

References

Burns, K., Ewers, C. L., and Ewers, E. (Directors). 2018. *The Mayo Clinic* [Motion Picture].

Carson, B. 1990. *Gifted Hands*. Grand Rapids, MI: Zondervan.

Eldredge, J. 2016. Moving Mountains. Nashville, TN: Nelson Books.Harris,

W. S., Gowda, M., Kolb, J. W., Strychacz, C. P., Vacek, J. L., Jones, P. P., . . . McCallister, B. D.1999. "A Randomized, Controlled Trial of the Effects of Remote Intercessory Prayer on Outcomes in Patients Admitted to the Coronary Care Unit." *Archives of Internal Medicine, 159:* 2273–78.

Keener, C. S. 2011. Miracles (Vol. 1). Grand Rapids, MI: Baker Academic.

Kelly, P., and Tazbir, J. 2014. *Essentials of Nursing Leadership and Management* (3rd ed.). Clifton Park, NY: Delmar.

Kendrick, A., and Kendrick, S. (2015). *The Battle Plan for Prayer*. Nashville, TN: B&H Books.

Mamier, I., Ricci-Allegra, P., Foith, J., and Taylor, E. J. 2017. "Self-reported Frequency of

Nurse-provided Spiritual Care." *Applied Nursing Research* 30–35.

Matthews, D. A., Marlowe, S. M., and McNutt, F. S. 2001. "Effects of Intercessory Prayer on Patients with Rheumatoid Arthritis." Southern Medical Journal, 12(93): 1177-88.

Omartian, S. (2014). *The Power of a Praying Wife*. Eugene, OR: Harvest House Publishers.

Phillips, S. W. 2006. *Just in Time! Pastoral Prayers for the Hospital Visit*. TN: Abingdon Press.

Saliman, G. 2010. "The Prayer Prescription." The Permanente Journal 14(1): 41–45. Sanford, A. 2017. The Healing Light. Oxford: Benediction Classics.

Selby, D., Seccaraccia, D., Huth, J., Kurrpa, K., and Fitch, M. 2016. "A Qualitative Analysis of a Healthcare Professional's Understanding and Approach to Management of Spiritual Distress." *Journal of Palliative Medicine* 19(11): 1197–1204.

"Serpent." Biblical Training. (2020, January 19). Serpent. Retrieved from Biblical Training: https://www.biblicaltraining.org/library/serpent

Stroble, L. 2018. *The Case for Miracles*. Grand Rapids, MI: Zondervan.

The Blue Letter Bible. 2019. www.blueletterbible.org

Wynne, L. 2013. "Spiritual Care at the End of Life." *Nursing Standard* 2(28): 41-45.

Zodhiates, S., and Baker, W. D. 1991. Key Work Study Bible. Chattanooga, TN: AMG International, Inc.

Zollfrank, A. A., Trevino, K. M., Cadge, W., Balboni, M. J., Thiel, M. M., Fitchett, G., and Balboni, T. A. 2015. "Teaching Health Care Workers to Provide Spiritual Care: A Pilot Study." *Journal of Palliative Medicine* 5(18), 408–415. doi:10.1089/jpm.2014.0306

About the Author

Jennifer R. Buettner, RN, BSN, CEN, is a talented nurse, educator, wife, and mother. She began her writing career as a successful author of the popular ER nursing book, *Fast Facts for the ER Nurse* published by Springer Publishing. Her medical career progressed from a hospital volunteer, then patient care technician, LPN, RN, preceptor, charge nurse, and nurse educator. As a Georgia State University graduate with over two decades of emergency nursing experience, she has spent several years writing, precepting, teaching, and serving as a legal nurse consultant. She holds numerous nursing instructor and professional certifications. Jennifer currently serves as an Education Coordinator for an Emergency Department at Emory Healthcare system in Atlanta, Georgia. In her role, Mrs. Buettner works to advance the careers of emergency nurses through education and evidence-based practice. Jennifer also serves at her local church, children's school, and local community. She finds great joy in helping others grow professionally and cultivating their inner gifts and talents.

It wasn't until much later in her nursing career that Jennifer discovered a way to combine her nursing expertise and natural gift of writing to serve and bring glory to God. *When a Nurse Prays* is a declaration of her faith that encompasses all her passions and God-given talents. On her days off, she enjoys painting, a good cup of tea, a good book, and sunshine on the front porch. Jennifer and her husband, Nick, live in Georgia and enjoy spending time with their children, friends, and family. Through her writing she has grown closer to the Lord and hopes her work will encourage others to reflect the love of God through prayer.

Printed in the United States
by Baker & Taylor Publisher Services